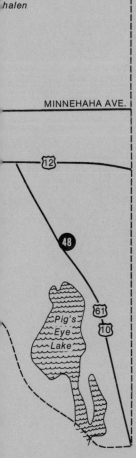

Drawings*

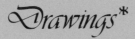

Neighborhoods

* Complete list of drawings with page numbers follows table of contents.

The Twin Cities Perceived

A Study in Words and Drawings

The Twin Cities Perceived

A Study in Words and Drawings

Text by Jean Adams Ervin

Drawings by
Gemma Rossini Cullen, Robert Halladay,
Heidi Schwabacher, and Robert N. Taylor

The University of Minnesota Press,

Minneapolis

Library of Congress Catalog Card Number 76-7338

ISBN 0-8166-0786-9

The excerpt from John Berryman's poetry is reprinted with the permission of Farrar, Straus & Giroux, Inc., from *Recovery* by John Berryman, Foreword by Saul Bellow; copyright © 1973 by the Estate of John Berryman, Foreword copyright © 1973 by Saul Bellow. The excerpt from *The Letters of F. Scott Fitzgerald* is reprinted with permission of Charles Scribner's Sons; copyright © 1963 by Frances Scott Fitzgerald Lanahan. The excerpt from W. H. Auden's *The Age of Anxiety* is reprinted with the permission of Random House, Inc.; copyright © 1947 by W. H. Auden and renewed 1975 by Monroe K. Spears and William Meredith, Executors of the Estate of W. H. Auden. Permission for it was also given by Faber and Faber Ltd., publishers of W. H. Auden's *Collected Longer Poems*.

Preface

The long-time resident of the Twin Cities may consider a book on the visual characteristics of St. Paul and Minneapolis a superfluity, but the familiar object is often the one least clearly seen. Not only does "beauty soon grow familiar to the lover, fade in his eye and pall upon the sense," to adapt Joseph Addison's words, but ugliness too has a way of disappearing with time. For the reader whose sight is filmed over by familiarity our aim has been to throw a fresh light upon Minneapolis and St. Paul, and for the newcomer or prospective visitor, to give an overview that presents something of the variety to be encountered. The chauvinist who thinks that the Twin Cities are the prettiest places in the world will be jolted by some things in this book. At the other end of the spectrum those readers who see nothing but a wasteland of the middle way should look again. We hope that every reader will be inspired to take a new look at both Minneapolis and St. Paul. Many residents of one city never set foot into the other, and even for the more adventurous urban explorers the sheer size of the two cities is defeating. Minneapolis covers fifty-eight square miles; St. Paul, fifty-five. Therefore we hope to introduce the reader to relatively unknown gems such as the Justus Ramsey House, a tiny stone building dating from the 1850s in St. Paul, the Crosby Farm Park area, a newly developed wilderness along the Mississippi in St. Paul, the beautiful fountains in Lyndale Park near Minneapolis's Lake Harriet, and the onion-domed St. Mary's Russian Orthodox Greek Catholic Church in Minneapolis.

With the proliferation of photographic books, it might be asked why it was decided to use drawings for illustrations. The point is that an artist can often extract the essence of a scene or a building in a drawing in a way that photography cannot. Although I chose the subjects, each artist gives a highly individual interpretation, contributing to a memorable kaleidoscope of Minneapolis and St. Paul. Gemma Rossini Cullen, Robert Halladay, Heidi Schwabacher, and Robert N. Taylor brought to this book many years of experience working in various artistic media as well as a serious interest in the Twin Cities.

In any book of this nature there will be two cardinal sins, that of omission and the sin of commission. For the resident who has favorite areas, by far the more serious sin will be the first, but since it was impossible to discuss every neighborhood and section the best solution seemed to be a selection which was representative of each of the two cities. A mixture of old and new, of varying architectural styles and topographical features, was the goal. Inevitably, subjectivity played a large part, and therefore I wish to declare the highly personal nature of the book.

Throughout, references are made to historic sites and districts. Some buildings or districts may be on one or more historic registers. The National Register of Historic Places identifies historic resources, provides for possible preservation assistance, and requires that an appropriate body comment when there are threats to the preservation of the resources. The Minnesota legislation concerning historic sites and districts is more extensive. It protects sites from change in their historic character with-out the approval of the Minnesota Historical Society, provides for possible financial assistance in preserving sites, and enables subdivisions of the state to create commissions with zoning and other powers which would protect historic districts. The Minneapolis Heritage Preservation Commission recommends to the city council historic designation of buildings and districts which are worthy of preservation. If this designation is approved, no permits can be granted for construction, destruction, or alteration of the designated area without a review by the Heritage Preservation Commission.

Whether the aspect you are looking at is historic or not, most of the Twin Cities (I except the assembly-line features that are found in every American conurbation) is deserving of a second look. You may, as I have, cast a critical eye on some of it, while praising the rest. But this book is an effort to provide meaning, context, a frame of reference, and—not least of all—a stimulus and challenge to perception.

Jean Adams Ervin

Contents

List of Drawings

The Twin Cities Perceived

A Study in Words and Drawings

View from Harriet Island Marina, St. Paul, looking toward Cathedral.

Time and the River

Atop a commanding hill in St. Paul the Roman Catholic Cathedral announces itself in baroque grandeur, and the fortunate choice of this site is evident as you move from one area of the city to another only to realize that the Cathedral follows you around. In contrast, Minneapolis's most assertive building, the IDS Tower, must make its statement by thrusting itself fifty-seven stories into the air from exceedingly flat land. The placement of these two buildings tells us much of the physiognomy of these two cities.

St. Paul's stately Summit Avenue runs from the Mississippi River to a majestic ridge crowned by a fine group of nineteenth- and twentieth-century homes. But cliff-dwelling is not limited to privileged St. Paulites. The West Side community ranges from the flood plain of the river to the top of a steep escarpment. The streets of the Dayton's Bluff neighborhood clamber up and around confusingly. East Seventh Street, the backstairs entrance to downtown St. Paul, swoops upon the city from a considerable height. The most histrionic area is Highwood on the southeastern edge of the city, where residential streets twist, curve, and plunge through deep woods and open fields. Most of its homes are near or on a very high plateau with a fine view of the valley far below. In St. Paul the resident always seems about to ascend or descend.

Like most generalizations, the one that Minneapolis is a city bereft of hills must be qualified. The flat-chested sister is not really so uninteresting topographically, but is only apparently so when looked at alongside her more curvaceous sibling. Tower Hill in Southeast Minneapolis, one of the highest points in the city, is capped by a charming witch's hat water tower which has been patched and shored to nourish the sentiments of local residents, but it also serves as a landmark which, like the Cathedral, can be seen from a number of points in the cities. St. Anthony Boulevard winds its way through Northeast Minneapolis to Deming Heights with its hillside park. In the central part of the city, Lowry Hill has long attracted wealthy residents because of its fine lookout and Theodore

11

Tower Hill in the Prospect Park neighborhood, Minneapolis,
one of the highest points in the city.

Wirth Park boasts views from its hills of the distant downtown area. But these are not the dramatically steep areas that can be found in St. Paul. Much of Minneapolis was originally prairie and its general flatness attests to this.

It has been suggested that St. Paul and Minneapolis should be regarded as Siamese twins since their residential and industrial areas have long since grown together over their boundaries, but the image of fraternal twins is more apt, for Minneapolis with a 1975 estimate of 416,864 residents is 116,173 larger. Both cities cover a large geographical area, Minneapolis fifty-eight square miles and St. Paul fifty-five. Their genetic makeup is similar in many respects, but there are differences.

Flying over St. Paul and Minneapolis makes several things apparent. There are no mountains nearby so that although the surrounding countryside is somewhat barren of striking vistas the cities have had no natural barriers to their weedlike growth. The population pressures felt in other parts of the country are experienced as nudges here. Minneapolitans and St. Paulites have not been panicked into cutting down trees, sacrificing greenery to condominiums. Driving through the cities or flying over them in the summer, one is impressed with their lush green cover, a cover rent by lakes and ponds. The mixture of pastoral and urban elements in the midst of a metropolis is a principal feature. You grit your teeth at the effluvia of a Lake Street "where the used cars live," as John Berryman put it, but a few blocks away you can walk into a forest along the Mississippi River.

Roughly 11,000 years ago the last glacier retreated from Minnesota, leaving more than the 10,000 lakes touted in state publicity, a number of beautiful streams, and rolling hills. The glaciers carved the physiognomy of the two cities, making St. Paul into a relief map of canyons but giving to Minneapolis the lion's share of lakes. Geographically, Minneapolis and St. Paul are part of the hill and lake region of Minnesota, a quietly undulating, seldom startling area. The Twin Cities lack the drama of cliff-framed, sea-washed cities such as San Francisco and Naples, or of mountain-rimmed enclaves such as Mexico City. This is quiet theater, Chekhovian drama as opposed to Shakespeare.

From a plane another aspect becomes visible. The downtown areas are widely separated, by a distance of some nine miles, and if one city died tomorrow the other could exist without it. In most matters discrete city council governments still chart the fate of citizens, although St. Paul and Minneapolis are now part of the purview of a widely applauded Metropolitan Council which embraces a seven-county region. The Metropolitan Council was established in 1967 to deal with social and physical problems that have regional impact. The council reviews plans of such agencies as the Metropolitan Airports Commission, the Metropolitan Transit Commission, and the Metropolitan Sewer Board.

I should hesitate to call the Twin Cities' climatic polarity a Dr. Jekyll-Mr. Hyde dichotomy, but there is a vast difference in the personalities of the cities in summer and winter. The cold itself is legendary, but the look of the cities in winter probably affects residents as much as the actual temperatures. The stripped trees are not the same trees as those jungly summer creatures. Winter's most beautiful days can vie with summer's aesthetically when an ice storm leaves a cobwebby, dreamlike mist. Then the ice melts and it is a black and white Eugene Larkin print. Then comes a fresh snowfall

Looking upriver from the banks of the Mississippi River toward downtown Minneapolis.

13

and yesterday's morose onlooker becomes the most ardent devotee of Minnesota winters. The sun turns it all into a walker's paradise. This perpetual trickery goes on: two days later it is gray pepper sprinkled over the sugar bowl and, within a week, a mud pie of grimy snow, much harsher than good clean spring dirt.

March comes and the thermometer takes an unexpected plunge; we are swathed in our late winter drab for weeks perhaps. April makes a tentative appearance and suicide calls to crisis centers reach a crescendo every year. Children hunt for Easter eggs in the snow. And the wind lays on an extra prop in this absurd theater of the seasons so that the wind-chill factor may bring April 10 to below zero again. And the last, last blizzard is lurking in the wings.

Those who do not live here tend to romanticize Minnesota winters. Children slide, everyone skates, the flames in the fireplace warm. But much of it is less than glamorous. It is a sorry picture of potholes in the streets; of electric cords stretched to keep pet cars warm on the street; of the stuck car doing a samba when it starts to move, then alternating between a stately and a spastic dance; of the glassed-in front porch and the snow rake to prevent leaking roofs. Twin Citians really look different in the extremities of the seasons. They seem to change from antelope to buffalo. In winter they walk with their heads down, two eyes out for ice traps.

Essentially St. Paul and Minneapolis are no different from any other northern city. They take off their dress clothes and winter shows them warts and all, but they go around in their less flattering undress for a longer period than most areas. The railroads are more visible. The essentially unimagi-native architecture grinds its way into one's sensibility. Do they really have more ugly bars, gasoline stations, and billboards than other cities? Their misfortune is to have a longer period in which to contemplate it all in its nakedness.

Summer often starts the day after winter ends. The flamboyancies of winter weather are, though somewhat moderated, continued in the summer months. June is the rainy month and the cities burst into an outdoor greenhouse. Once more amnesia sets in when the tropical growth of trees in the cities nearly obliterates the sky in some sections. Twin Citians feel the most blessed of creatures. Trees hide bald spots and, like a well-cut suit on a paunchy gentleman, do wonders for the appearance. Then July lays on a steambath of ninety-degree weather for a ten-day stretch, but sometimes the thermometer hovers around forty-two degrees for days.

In both cities most residential areas are models of hand-clipped, manicured lawns, with perfectly trimmed bushes and brimming with flowers. Abstinence does indeed make the heart grow fonder here; for residents work hard to nurture every plant in this short growing season. Yards are often very small, but this never deters the domestic horticulturist. In fact, it often seems that the smaller the space for greening, the more bushes, trees, and flowers are apt to be jammed into it. Streets become cathedrallike naves of trees.

The cities really come into their own in early September. The hardiest of chrysanthemums continue to bloom for some weeks, often until early November; trees slowly shed their leaves, and the colors change. Their true riches—space, greenery, water, and sky—work together. The cloudless, deep blue sky, the brilliant maple, the more subtle elm and oak leaves, the wild grapevines climbing over a collapsing snow fence, and the sumac in a city yard remind us that we are not far from wilderness in either space or time.

The Mississippi River, the heart of the cities' heartland, is the best place from which to watch the seasons. In winter it is a frightening leviathan, framed in crepuscular tones. In spring the constantly changing highlights of foam—caused by organic matter in high water—are the most telling indices of its power. Here and there along the banks, trees and bushes put out tentative leaves to test the doubtful air. Summer creates a new river, one that sparkles between lush green banks in the gorge area. Autumn brings to the palette few mists but much mellow fruitfulness. Each of these *vedute* seems projected by a magic lantern and even today in unspoiled areas within the cities we can imagine the sight that greeted Minnesota's early explorers.

"For more than a hundred and fifty years there had been white settlements on our Atlantic coasts. These people were in intimate communication with the Indians: in the south the Spaniards were robbing, slaughtering, enslaving, and converting them; higher up, the English were trading beads and blankets to them for a consideration, and throwing in civilization and whiskey, 'for lagniappe'; and in Canada the French were schooling them in a rudimentary way, missionarying among them, and drawing whole populations of them at a time to Quebec, and later to Montreal, to buy furs of them. Necessarily, then, these various clusters of whites must have heard of the great river of the Far West; and indeed they did hear of it vaguely—so vaguely and indefinitely that its course, proportions, and locality were hardly even guessable. The mere mysteriousness of the matter ought to have

fired curiosity and compelled exploration; but this did not occur. Apparently, nobody happened to want such a river, nobody needed it, nobody was curious about it; so, for a century and a half the Mississippi remained out of the market and undisturbed. When De Soto found it, he was not hunting for a river, and had no present occasion for one; consequently, he did not value it or even take any particular notice of it.

"But at last, LaSalle, the Frenchman, conceived the idea of seeking out that river and exploring it. It always happens that when a man seizes upon a neglected and important idea, people inflamed with the same notion crop up all around. It happened so in this instance.

"Naturally the question suggests itself, Why did these people want the river now when nobody had wanted it in the five preceding generations? Apparently it was because at this late date they thought they had discovered a way to make it useful; for it had come to be believed that the Mississippi emptied into the Gulf of California, and therefore afforded a short cut from Canada to China."

Mark Twain's wry oversimplifications of history in *Life on the Mississippi* do nevertheless point to several facts more pungently than straightforward accounts. His imagery of the "Great River" as a commodity to be traded on the market highlights a fundamental geographic fact of the Twin Cities: they are here largely because the Mississippi River is here. St. Paul, the leading commercial center of the Northwest by the 1860s, grew up because it was the northern limit to steam navigation on the river. Upriver, the power of St. Anthony Falls, the most abrupt drop in the river from its beginnings at Lake Itasca to its mouth at the Gulf of Mexico,

15

was responsible for the birth of Minneapolis.

The river attracted its share of colorful adventurers whose hyperbolic accounts far exceeded Twain's poetic license. At the junction of Hennepin Avenue, Wayzata Boulevard, and Lyndale Avenue in Minneapolis today there stands a statue of a benign-looking friar of the Franciscan Recollect Order whose descriptions went beyond even hyperbole. Father Louis Hennepin, who had come to the New World as a missionary, was invited by LaSalle to accompany his western expedition as chaplain, but was packed off to explore the upper Mississippi when LaSalle could no longer bear his mendacious braggadocio. With Michel Accault and Antoine Auguelle, Hennepin was to ascertain the navigability of the upper Mississippi for sailing vessels. During several months when they were in the hands of the Sioux, Hennepin apparently was the first white man to see the magnificent falls. On his return to Europe Hennepin wrote three runaway best sellers, largely embroideries on his North American adventures, but historians have agreed that he did at least name the Falls of St. Anthony for his order's patron saint, St. Anthony of Padua.

Later visitors were enthralled by the sight of the falls.

"Seated on the top of an elevated promontory, I see, at half a mile distance, two great masses of water unite at the foot of an island which they encircle, and whose majestic trees deck them with the loveliest hues, in which all the magic play of light and shade are reflected on their brilliant surface. From this point they rush down a rapid descent about two hundred feet long, and, breaking against the scattered rocks which obstruct their passage, they spray up and dash together in a thousand varied forms. They then fall into a transverse basin, in the form of a cradle, and are urged upwards by the force of gravitation against the side of the precipice, which seems to stop them a moment only to encrease the violence with which they fling themselves down a depth of twenty feet. The rocks against which these great volumes of water dash, throw them back in white foam and glittering spray; then, plunging into the cavities which this mighty fall has hollowed, they rush forth again in tumultuous waves, and once more break against a great mass of sandstone forming a little island in the midst of their bed, on which two thick maples spread their shady branches.

"This is the spot called the Falls of St. Anthony, eight miles above the fort. . . . A mill and a few little cottages, built by the colonel for the use of the garrison, and surrounding country adorned with romantic scenes complete the magnificent picture."

Thus wrote Giacomo Beltrami to his friend the Countess Giulia Medici-Spada in 1823. Beltrami, a political exile from Venice, traveled west to the Mississippi like so many adventurous Europeans of his day. When he reached the confluence of the Ohio and Mississippi rivers, Beltrami intended to proceed to New Orleans and Mexico. But on the first boat Beltrami could catch going to St. Louis, *The Calhoun*, he met Major Lawrence Taliaferro, an Indian agent on his way to Fort St. Anthony, later renamed Fort Snelling. Intrigued by Taliaferro's descriptions of Indian life and of the beauty of the surroundings, Beltrami impulsively switched plans and thus became the first modern tourist in Minnesota. The boat on which he traveled to Fort St. Anthony, *The Virginia*, was the first steamboat to make the dangerous trip to the farthest navigable point on the upper Mississippi. Beltrami's exuberant romanticizing of the Indians and the landscape was symbolically reflected in his foppish red umbrella, which he continued to carry in spite of less than Continental luxury on the boat, continual delays while *The Virginia* was being extricated from sandbars, and at one point his being lost on shore in the woods. Minnesota's tourist industry was pioneered by a gentleman with a whim of iron.

It was the artist George Catlin who proposed the idea of a fashionable tour of the upper Mississippi some dozen years later, drawing attention to the "magnificence of the scenes which are continually opening to the eye of the traveller and riveting him to the deck of the steamer through sunshine, lightning or rain, from the mouth of the Ouisconsin to the Fall of St. Anthony."

Within a decade Catlin's idea took root and a tour of the upper Mississippi attracted travelers from New Orleans and St. Louis and as far away as New York and Washington. In 1862 the English novelist Anthony Trollope wrote, "I protest that of all the river scenery that I know, that of the Upper Mississippi is by far the finest and the most continued. One thinks of course of the Rhine; but, according to my idea of beauty, the Rhine is nothing to the Upper Mississippi. For miles upon miles, for hundreds of miles, the course of the river runs through low hills, which are there called bluffs. These bluffs rise in every imaginable form, looking sometimes like large straggling unwieldy castles, and then throwing themselves into sloping lawns which stretch back away from the river, till the eye is lost in their twists and turnings. . . . There are no high mountains, but there is a succession of hills which group themselves forever without monotony. . . . The idea constantly occurs that some point on every hillside would form the most

charming site ever yet chosen for a noble residence."

For those who liked to rough it in a civilized way the steamboats provided music and dancing and frequently a side trip to Fort Snelling and to the falls of St. Anthony and Minnehaha, which the effusive Beltrami compared to the waterfalls of the Villa d'Este in Tivoli. To promote the upper Mississippi, lecturers in eastern cities illustrated their talks by slowly unrolling long sheets of painted

Heidi Schwabacher

A tug-pushed barge going downriver through the Mississippi River gorge.

17

canvas with views of the river and the life along its banks. And today a trip through the Twin Cities along or on the river unrolls a modern panorama of the cities. The river not only gives back a literal reflection of life on its banks but is a microcosm of Minneapolis and St. Paul, for it is both a pastoral retreat and an industrial wasteland.

The upper Mississippi from the mouth of the Missouri River north, which so fascinated Trollope, Catlin, and Beltrami, was a dangerous and capricious highway, turbulent in floodtime, but in places too shallow to navigate in a drought. During the nineteenth and early twentieth centuries channels were dug to accommodate barge traffic, but with the development of the diesel-powered tug which is capable of pushing a dozen or more steel barges, a nine-foot channel was needed to assure continuous navigation in a drought. The channel was completed in 1963, having been some thirty years in the making. The lock at St. Anthony Falls is the top plank in the "Mississippi Stairway," a sequence of channels connected by locks and dams which allow barge traffic to flourish from Minneapolis to St. Louis. The St. Anthony lock has a lift of forty-nine feet, a frightening cavern to look into.

Barge traffic is the most visible link with the past; by 1866 barges were being used to carry grain downstream, but with the coming of the railroads, and until the nine-foot channel was dug, the river traffic suffered a decline. But with the completion of the nine-foot channel, there has been a renaissance of traffic. Between the months of April and December any watcher on the river will be rewarded with the sight of these seemingly prehistoric monsters moving downstream with grain or upstream with coal and chemicals. The increase in traffic is not without its problems: potential spill-age of chemicals has worried conservationists and deposits of sand and mud from continual dredging can cause sterilization of the rich backwaters of the Mississippi with ominous ramifications for its ecological balance.

But as a visual matter the barge represents one commercial use of the river which retains an aura of adventure. While the tugs are a far cry from the glamorous steamers of the nineteenth century, they have their own attractive, jaunty air. From the river bluffs the tug-pushed barges look like great sea turtles in their apparently effortless movement, but a canoeist on the river comes to respect their frightening power, for watching the approach of a barge is rather like feeling about to be engulfed by a glacier. Freeways and railroads crisscrossing the cities have all but obliterated our memory of the Mississippi as the main highway to both St. Paul and Minneapolis, but for many decades it was the lifeline for exploration, trade, immigration, and settlement of the inland empire.

The observation deck at the St. Anthony Falls lock is a vantage point from which we can see not only down the great staircase of the Mississippi but back into history. Here the first hydroelectric plant in the United States was built in 1882. Across the river is the spire of Our Lady of Lourdes, a graceful Italian Romanesque church, the oldest continuously used church in Minneapolis. Near it is the Pillsbury A Mill, designed by L. S. Buffington, from the 1880s until 1930 one of the largest flour mills in the world. A Florentine palazzo with a concave façade in rock-faced limestone, it is a handsome building as well as a reminder of the milling empire which grew up on these banks. Today the A Mill is used for packing and warehousing. Throughout the cities we are confronted with more familiar monu-

Robert Halladay

Pillsbury A Mill, Main Street Southeast, Minneapolis.

Robert Halladay

Pracna on Main, 117 Main Street Southeast, Minneapolis, within the St. Anthony Historic District.
Built in 1890, the Pracna building has been handsomely refurbished as a restaurant.

ments to the flour-milling industry, the grain storage bins rising in simple dignity. The renovation of Southeast Main Street adjacent to the Pillsbury A Mill is a partial re-creation of the city of St. Anthony which was the twin to Minneapolis across the river until they were consolidated in 1872.

Immediately to the rear of the observation deck loom the storage bins on the west bank, which can be regarded as our castles on the new Rhine. These quiet sentinels stand on the site of one of the worst milling tragedies, the explosion of the Washburn Mill in 1878, caused by flour dust and gases. Eighteen men were killed and nearby buildings destroyed.

Today the Falls of St. Anthony are a muted reminder of their days of glory when visitors such as

20

George Catlin, Jonathan Carver, and Seth Eastman were inspired to paint them. But from the 1820s until the early twentieth century they were used to power the wheels of the lumber and flour mills directly, and as is so often the case, their usefulness was their undoing, for by the 1860s the burgeoning mills and dams had begun to make haggard this once-fresh natural beauty. For thousands of years the falls had been moving upstream from Fort Snelling at an average rate of 2.44 feet per year, cutting the magnificent river gorge. The natural erosion and even more unnatural strains put upon the falls by industry forced the building of an apron over them so that their retreat was permanently halted. But even today in a springtime of particularly high waters, the falls take on a semblance of their early days, turning into a huge cappuccino-colored torrent.

The Mississippi was spanned for the first time in 1854 at Nicollet Island, and a handsome suspension bridge there was a local trademark until the 1870s when it was demolished as unsafe. In its day Nicollet Island has been a tatterdemalion half-overgrown with bushes, weeds, rundown and abandoned homes, and some industry. Once-fine residences such as the Grove Street Flats remind us that this was a fashionable area in earlier times. During prohibition, gambling speakeasies were run by local Al Capones. Later the island became a hangout for winos and a drop-off point for murder victims and the home of charitable institutions such as the Salvation Army and the Harvest Field Mission. Now these groups have been moved along and this historic waif is undergoing some renovation as part of the St. Anthony Historic District.

If the grain elevators are the Rhine castles, the stone arch railroad bridge asserting itself diagonal-ly across the river near the falls is the Roman viaduct. It is a further indication that some of the handsomest structures remaining from the nineteenth century are those built for commerce, often far more expressive than the Victorian Gothic castles built by men whose pockets overflowed from running these industries. The bridge—"Jim Hill's Folly," as it was called when plans for its construction were announced in 1881—is a handsome legacy whose eastern end is not far from the A Mill. Near that end a series of board steps takes the hiker down the precipitous green riverbank, and from a number of points along this jungle within the city the walker, looking up at the bridge, is made aware of man's own counterchallenge to the majestic natural highway. Great limestone blocks were formed into a series of graceful catenary arches at the climax of the journey bringing the wheat from the Northwest to the burgeoning flour mills at the falls.

When Hill arrived in St. Paul in 1856 Minneapolis and St. Anthony were upstream upstarts while St. Paul was the leading commercial center of the Northwest. The heart of the center was the lower levee at the foot of Jackson Street. In those days St. Paul was said to look like a city of steamboats; in 1858 1,090 boats were registered at her wharves. Significantly, the great years of steamboating on the upper Mississippi began with the creation of Minnesota Territory, opening the lands of the upper Mississippi Valley to settlement. And it was fitting that the river played its role histrionically in that auspicious year of 1849. Lake Pepin had been frozen for five months. When Captain Daniel Harris, the colorful steamboat master, forced his way through the ice and rounded the bend below St. Paul, a flash of lightning revealed his *Dr. Franklin*

#2 which carried the news that Minnesota was now a territory. For the next twenty years land-hungry Europeans and Americans jammed the steamboats from New Orleans, St. Louis, and Galena.

The slaughter of thousands of people every year on our highways may lead us to romanticize the slow-moving steamboat, but these quaint vessels, often tarted up with gingerbread carving and bright paint, were in reality deathtraps that frequently exploded, caught fire, or were sunk by tornadoes. Cholera, lack of sanitation, poor food, and overcrowding added to the list of dangers for the lower deck passenger; and the river attracted its share of flimflam types who preyed upon the innocents.

But the steamboats were the cheapest and most efficient mode of transportation until the coming of the railroads in the 1870s. They were the bringer of food, news, fun. In his *Steamboating on the Upper Mississippi* William Petersen has remarked that "the ultima thule of spring navigation was St. Paul at the head of navigation on the Upper Mississippi. Each spring the mad dash of steamboats for this port was chronicled by the press all the way up from St. Louis."

It might be expected that so valuable and beautiful a gift of nature as the Mississippi would be covered by a protective casing of laws and that we would wear our company manners near it, treating the river as our front parlor where we show our best to the world. But unfortunately it is here that we let it all hang out. Biologists have dubbed the river "the colon of Mid-America." And no wonder. Industrial and human waste, barge washing, and storm sewers have contributed to the prostitution of this once great beauty. The Mississippi and its banks in Minneapolis and St. Paul today offer some of the most beautiful stretches of water and land in Minnesota and some of the ugliest. The river watcher marvels at bluffs of incomparable beauty, as the river takes its graceful course through the virtual forest land of the gorge. But immediately north of this area, beneath the Washington Avenue bridge in Minneapolis, oil storage tanks in "screaming white" flank one embankment (recently converted to a city park!).

Even more appalling, in northern Minneapolis scrap-iron companies sprawl over acres of land between Washington Avenue North and the river. Railroads and industry still corrode much of the riverfront land on both sides in the central river area of Minneapolis, although many of the tracks are no longer used. The railroads followed the flour and lumber industries and in turn attracted other industries. Now there is no particular reason for their existence on the river, for lumber milling died out many years ago and there is little flour milling on the river today. The large industrial complex could have been moved elsewhere long since. It is rather like a group of soldiers and campfollowers spawning a whole generation of illegitimate children who remain on many years after the war has ended.

A drive downriver along Shepard Road leads past the marker for the historic Fountain Cave. The cave identified the site of the first building in what is now St. Paul, the hovel put up by Pig's Eye Parrant, purveyor of illegal whisky to Indians and soldiers. Mark Twain, ever perceptive, notes in *Life on the Mississippi*: "How solemn and beautiful is the thought that the earliest pioneer of civilization, the van-leader of civilization, is never the steamboat, never the railroad, never the newspaper, never the Sabbath-school, never the missionary—but always whisky! . . . This great van-leader ar-

Robert Halladay

Stone Arch Bridge in Minneapolis.

Scrap metal junkyards, Shepard Road, St. Paul.

rived upon the ground which St. Paul now occupies in June, 1837. Yes, at that date, Pierre Parrant, a Canadian, built the first cabin, uncorked his jug, and began to sell whisky to the Indians. The result is before us."

The beautiful Fountain Cave, with its sandstone walls and a stream flowing through its chambers, was Parrant's neighbor. Over the years, debris gradually filled it in, and in 1960 it was completely closed off, a victim of highway building. Continuing on Shepard into the commercial core of St. Paul, the driver passes the frightfully ironic comment on the end product of "the progress" that blotted out Fountain Cave, for here, near the foot of the High Bridge, is a car graveyard where the dead are not even decently buried. Near downtown

St. Paul, railroad tracks, oil storage tanks, and coal mounds parallel the river, and across the water there is a profusion of commerce and industry which almost obscures the breathtaking cliffs of the West Side. Harriet Island once had superb public baths which became the victims of the encroachment of filthy river water. Navy Island is an enormous car park, featuring a nightclub.

In eastern St. Paul Indian Mounds Park offers a telling juxtaposition of prehistory and modern life, urban and rural worlds. These hillocks were repositories of dead Indians and their possessions. Archaeological excavations of Indian mounds throughout the region which have turned up arrowheads, pottery, copper pieces, and other artifacts have told us much about the lives of the first Americans. A short distance from Mounds Park is a marker for Carver's Cave, discovered in the bluffs in 1766 by Jonathan Carver while he was searching for a Northwest Passage to the Pacific Ocean. The cave had an entrance ten feet wide and five feet high, and there was a lake some twenty feet from its entrance. Indian pictographs carved into the soft sandstone were still visible in the late nineteenth century, but several hundred feet of the bluffs were cut away at that time in order to accommodate the railroads and although the cave was reopened from 1913 until 1958 the accumulated debris forced its closing. The view from the park above is an indictment of all of our wanton disregard for such beauties. Hugh acreages of railroad tracks run close to the river's edge and across the river the Holman Airport sprawls along an enormous stretch of riverfront land which could be used for recreation.

But the river in the cities offers something other than the violent contrasts of unspoiled nature and absolute pollution. The view upriver from the Franklin Avenue Bridge in Minneapolis lays before us the healthy schizophrenia of life, for there a modern city rises. Franklin Avenue East features several anonymous high-rise apartment houses, further upstream there is the IDS Tower, and the old City-County Courthouse reminds us of the taste for Romanesque grandeur of earlier decades. On the river flats of the east bank the University of Minnesota showboat, the *General John Newton*, is moored picturesquely.

Downriver, there is a breathtaking lovely stretch of wilderness on the steep banks, where a gash is cut by the river to form a gorge. In some places the banks are a hundred feet high. Below them on both sides are large sand flats, and a railroad bridge is the only sign of the industrial world. On the west side a boy runs in wild abandon along the river's edge, another swings over the water on a rope, behind them a clifflike bank rises in a tangled jungle of greenery. It is still possible to plunge out of city life into the wilderness, provided one has alpine instincts and capabilities, for in most places you must descend by steep paths, clinging to roots until the flats are reached, although recently a few primitive wooden steps have improved this approach. Some all-too-graphic reminders of city life persist in the presence of the ubiquitous beer can, but otherwise it is easy to forget that you are in a large metropolitan area. Dense woodland, luxurious stretches of sand flats, low bushes, wild flowers, weeds, and the beautiful river make the arduous descent worthwhile. In the late autumn when the trees are bare, the limestone cliffs add another dimension to the rugged beauty. Walking to the north side of the Franklin Bridge you find one of the compelling wonders on the east bank,

Bridal Veil Falls, a cataract that can be heard long before it is seen even above the roar of bridge traffic. These powerful, yet diaphonous-appearing falls do indeed suggest a long misty veil, often embellished with a dramatic rainbow near the base.

Other falls can be found on both banks of the river. Southward in St. Paul are the Shadow Falls and Hidden Falls, and on the west bank at approximately East Twenty-sixth Street is another, unnamed waterfall. Hundreds of springs gush from the banks of the Mississippi, some of them nurturing watercress which often stays green all winter.

Near the west side of the Franklin Avenue Bridge a stone marks the beginning of the Winchell Trail running south along the river to Minnehaha Parkway. Named for N. H. Winchell, an eminent Minnesota geologist, it follows an old Indian trail, providing some of the most magnificent views of the river gorge. High wooded bluffs above sand flats blot out much of urban life, particularly where the trail dips down close to the river. The internal erosion of porous St. Peter sandstone by groundwater seepage known as "piping" has carved out a number of caves along the banks from St. Anthony Falls to Fort Snelling, although many have been covered in recent years since they constitute a danger to inexperienced speleologists.

Where Thirty-sixth Street meets the West River Road in Minneapolis one comes upon a steep ravine banked with limestone cliffs, in which birch and other deciduous trees grow, a deep pocket cut into the riverbank at right angles to the river. Adjacent to the ravine is a natural bowl containing the only virgin prairie within the cities. The prairie area provides a picture of the original vegetation found in this region, and in autumn the tall grass and red oaks turn into a mellow kaleidoscope of colors. Here the Winchell Trail rises to a natural viewing platform, a large mesalike area from which there is a widescreen panorama of the river gorge.

On the east side of the river the Mississippi Boulevard takes its apparently erratic course from the shape of the bluffs, offering constantly changing, ever striking views. The array of fine residences is interrupted by the Ford Assembly Plant, but if you turn your back upon that excrescence and look across the river you will see an interesting collection of late nineteenth- and early twentieth-century reform-school-style red-brick buildings which make up the campus of the Minnesota Veterans Home. Immediately to the north is the Ford Lock and Dam, and during the mild months crafts ranging in size from barges to canoes can be seen going through the lock. Looking at the west bank just behind the lock, you will see how the eroding action of the water has uncovered dramatic bluffs of Platteville limestone over white sandstone. The effect is rather like that of a slice of multilayered cake.

Throughout the cities are buildings fashioned from the rugged limestone, highly expressive structures which are some of our finest legacies from the nineteenth century. One of the loveliest is at 375 Mount Curve Boulevard, St. Paul, built in the 1860s by Frederick Spangenberg, a dairy farmer. A gracious home with simple lines, it resembles the Sibley and Faribault limestone homes in Mendota, the oldest homes in the state.

In 1805 the first American military expedition into what is now Minnesota was undertaken by twenty-six-year-old Lieutenant Zebulon Pike, sent to explore the upper reaches of the newly acquired Louisiana Territory. At the confluence of the Minnesota and Mississippi rivers, on Pike Island, the

American flag was raised for the first time in Minnesota. Pike secured nine miles on each side of the Mississippi from the Sioux, an acquisition that helped to fix the site of the first military post in Minnesota fifteen years later. High on the majestic bluffs above Pike Island the round tower in Fort St. Anthony was built in 1820, the first building erected by white Americans in Minnesota. Later renamed for its first commander, Colonel Josiah Snelling, the fort was the northwestern link in the chain of forts built to keep peace with the Indians and to counteract British influence among them. In addition, the fort was an important fur-trading depot. The magnitude of the task of policing 90,000 square miles can only be imagined today, but as we stand looking from the fort at the beauty of the river valleys, we can conjure up a semblance of the wonderment that young Pike must have experienced.

Although not dramatically beautiful, Pike Island holds its own as a relatively unspoiled area, fortunately secured as part of Fort Snelling State Park, with no automobile traffic allowed. Above it rugged banks ascend to the fort with its harshly outlined limestone buildings now restored to their nineteenth-century condition. The river watcher can easily get close to the water and gaze in mild surmise at two lovely rivers.

After the Civil War the river's importance was gradually superseded by the growth of the railroads, which took on the role of the primary agent in the distribution of farm and trade goods. Minneapolis and St. Paul became the transportation hub for Minnesota and much of the Middle West. At 240 Summit Avenue in St. Paul James J. Hill's arrogant mansion is a symbol of the might and extravagant carelessness of a whole race of empire

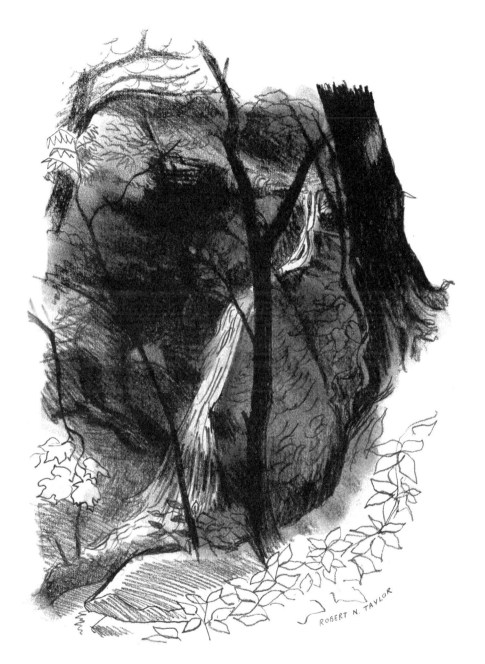

Shadow Falls Park, St. Paul.

Lock and Dam #1 near the Ford Bridge.

28

Fort Snelling, with Mendota Bridge in background, as seen from lookout on Mississippi River Boulevard, St. Paul.

builders. It was Hill who transformed the Northwest with his network of railroads. Railroad tracks scar the face of both cities, slashing back and forth, cutting through otherwise livable neighborhoods and parks, ruining walking areas, and, in the case of the large railroad marshaling yards, covering vast acreages. More than 5 percent of the built-up area of the cities is given over to railroads. Minneapolis was even more vulnerable than St. Paul since its high proportion of flat land made the building of tracks easy.

Railroad tracks are a psychological and social barrier, as effective as a Berlin Wall. In Minneapolis is one of the most achingly lovely spots to spend an afternoon walking, canoeing, or lolling. Canoeists can go from Lake Calhoun to Lake of the Isles

29

to Cedar Lake, but their enjoyment has long been interrupted by the shunting of boxcars across the tracks in an otherwise beautiful lagoon connecting Lake of the Isles to Cedar Lake. In Southeast Minneapolis, Van Cleve Park is much used by neighborhood families whose individual yards are small, but railroad tracks are dangerously close to the park and homes. In 1975 a high school student was fatally injured while taking a short cut across the tracks on his way to football practice. In Northeast Minneapolis, Deming Heights Park has an attractively steep hill with bike paths and an abundance of trees. But from here there is an all too clear view of the factories and a wasteland of railroad yards on the plain below. In St. Paul the Payne-Minnehaha area is called "railroad island" as it is bordered

ROBERT N. TAYLOR

Robert N. Taylor

*Although Minneapolis is no longer the flour milling center of the United States,
the grain storage bins and elevators still make a dramatic statement.*

31

by tracks on its east, west, and north sides and further west St. Anthony Park is cut into two emphatically separate neighborhoods by an enormous complex of railroad yards.

Tunneling under the campus of the University of Minnesota in Minneapolis are the Burlington Northern tracks. On March 24, 1975, at Fifteenth Avenue and Fourth Street Southeast, a road bridge which cut through a shopping area on the edge of the university campus collapsed when five freight cars derailed on a broken track, hitting a bridge support. Months of repair work and rerouted traffic snarled the entire area. Fortunately there were no casualties, but someone could well have been killed in such a heavily used shopping district, near a main artery.

The railroads made parts of the Twin Cities ugly before they were old, but some excuse can be offered for tracks and yards which existed before homes. Indeed, certain neighborhoods grew because of the proximity to railroad shops, in days before workers had adequate transportation to distant jobs. A more insidious example of poisoning the well of neighborhoods is the highway building in recent decades, bisecting neighborhoods and destroying a whole way of life in some cases.

In Prospect Park in Minneapolis a gem of a home designed by Frank Lloyd Wright in 1934 now overlooks the linear dungeon built for Interstate Highway 94. The attendant noise was so bad that the owners (who liked their home and the neighborhood) eventually moved to the suburbs. But as important as the effect on particular buildings of artistic and historic importance is the overall locustlike blight formed by the building of a highway. Twin Citians are justifiably proud of their civic participation, and in many achievements, particularly support for the performing arts, this is an impressive community. But warning bells failed to alert citizen groups before highways did their damage in the last few decades and neighborhoods are finding that former oases in the cities have become aural and visual nightmares.

Near the Mississippi in Minneapolis beautiful Riverside Park has frenzied freeway traffic along one of its boundaries. This park, which serves families of extremely modest incomes, is important for people whose outdoor living space is cramped. But now a walk in the park is ruined by the attendant roar. In the southeast quadrant of the Summit-University area of St. Paul a thriving black community with a history dating back to the 1880s was cut in half when I-94 was built. Sound barriers have been constructed in some areas, but too often they are Band-Aids applied after major surgery.

Drop here, with honor due, my trunk and brain
among the passioning of my countrymen
unable to read, rich, proud of their tags
and proud of me, Assemble all my bags!
Bury me in a hole, and give a cheer,
Near Cedar on Lake Street, where the
used cars live.

JOHN BERRYMAN

The Twin Cities' contribution to the glacial drift of our fast food-used car-sauna parlor-billboard culture has two brobdingnagian tentacles, one stretching along Lake Street in Minneapolis and the other along University Avenue from Minneapolis to downtown St. Paul through the Midway district. An archaeologist of the twenty-first century coming upon this seam of drift might well ponder—how could the inhabitants have been so hungry as to

warrant seven fast food emporiums within three blocks of one another? What gargantuan appetites their vehicles had for gasoline! And were they buying throwaway cars? Both areas feature that manifestation of modern purgatory, empty lots alternating with the ugliest new buildings, shopping centers in rural slum style, and cars, cars, cars on sale. There are almost no charming older buildings to take the sting out of it all.

The Midway, through which University Avenue runs, is one of the largest concentrations of trucking industries in the world and ironically this is one of the principal approaches to the State Capitol. Lake Street, once slated to be a major boulevard, connects the handsome West River Road with the Lake Calhoun/Lake of the Isles area. Lake Street and University Avenue are not the only blighted streets in St. Paul and Minneapolis, they are simply the most visible examples of the Twin Cities' surrender to the internal combustion engine.

Minneapolis and St. Paul are threaded with a number of boulevards and parkways, streets in part laid out with ample amounts of open spaces between the two one-way sections and often with a wide swatch of grass and trees at the sides. Middle westerners can consider them compensation for being born too late for the New England green, and although both cities grew too fast for orderly planning, subsequent boulevard development has at least made a virtue of the necessity of traffic. Summit Avenue in St. Paul, which runs four and one-half miles from the Cathedral to the Mississippi, is the best known of these boulevards. Lined in its early years along its eastern half with a succession of historically important mansions, it continued to be a sought-after district when smaller homes were built in subsequent decades.

Other, less affluent neighborhoods have been spruced up with boulevards such as Minnehaha, Stinson, Victory, North Xerxes, and St. Anthony in Minneapolis and Johnson, Lexington, Wheelock, and Ford parkways in St. Paul. On Victory Memorial Drive in Minneapolis American elm trees were planted to honor the servicemen killed in World War I, 600 of them named for particular soldiers and sailors. In both cities other residential streets are fairly wide and residents do not feel cramped as in many cities built in an earlier day. Unfortunately a large proportion of residential streets were laid out in a military grid plan, a system of platting cheapest for developers, but extremely dull visually. Even where the terrain is somewhat varied it tends to bring to one dead level every street, and in much of Minneapolis the saddest sort of anonymity sets in when street names are Thirty-second Avenue and Twenty-fifth Street, as though no one cared enough to find a name. In the summer the monotony of the grid plan is somewhat softened by the plethora of trees. Both cities reverse the usual pattern of a treeless inner city with garden suburbs beyond. Newer suburbs are often bereft of trees, while the cities have retained large old beautiful oaks and elms although the Dutch elm disease and oak wilt threaten their existence.

There are some exceptions to the military grid plans, amongst them the residential parks laid out in the nineteenth century—such as Macalester, Warrendale, and St. Anthony parks in St. Paul and Prospect, Oak, and Washburn parks in Minneapolis, where the streets were designed to follow the terrain—and although subsequent building has changed their aspects, these neighborhoods remain today proof of imagination in residential planning on a small scale.

Robert Halladay

West Calhoun Boulevard, Minneapolis. One of the many parkways and boulevards in the two cities.

Living Room

Architecturally neither St. Paul nor Minneapolis is particularly distinguished and it would be difficult to sort them out. Both have a vast amount of bungaloid drab, the one- or one-and-a-half-story home of the sort which flourished in the second and third decades of this century, crowded on a modest size lot. Usually there is a low pitched roof, with a porch or veranda in front, and a repeat gable on the main body of the home. The little house proliferated like the black-eyed susan in empty lots. Another version of the small middle western house, usually older than the bungalow, is the narrow frame house, with a steeply pitched roof, built to fit onto a thirty-foot lot, such as the workingmen's cottages on Milwaukee Avenue in Minneapolis. There are Tudorbethan stucco, half-timbered announcements of wealth along Summit Avenue in St. Paul and its counterparts in Kenwood, Lowry Hill, and Southwest Minneapolis. The middle western Spanish hacienda was particularly congenial to the 1920s and sprang up all over the more affluent sections of Minneapolis and St. Paul. Both cities have some elegant old homes, and although Minneapolis cannot point to such a concentration of imposing residences as those in the Historic Hill District of St. Paul, individual homes on Park Avenue and Lowry Hill match St. Paul's elegance. In both cities the glassed-in front porch allows the more modest dwelling to extend its living space for insanely long winters.

The Historic Hill District of St. Paul is one of the most extensive and intact assemblages of nineteenth- and early twentieth-century homes in the United States and is a microcosm of upper-middle- and upper-class homes to be found in both cities. Writing in 1891 Montgomery Schuyler, a perceptive architectural critic, observed that the fashionable quarter of St. Paul "could not have been established anywhere but at the edge of the bluff overhanging the town and commanding the Mississippi. . . . Indeed, there are very few streets in the United States that give in as high a degree as Summit Avenue the sense of an expenditure liberal

One of the stucco bungalows which proliferated
throughout Minneapolis and St. Paul.

without ostentation, directed by skill and restrained by taste. What mainly strikes a pilgrim from the East is not so much the merit of the best of these houses as the fact that there are no bad ones; none at least so bad as to disturb the general impression of richness and refinement and none that make the crude display of 'new money' that is to be seen in the fashionable quarters of cities even richer and far older."

The Historic Hill District has suffered a decline in certain areas and many homes were sold to non-profit institutions which were not subject to high taxes, but it has remained a well-appointed area since its inception, and has miraculously escaped the leveling influences of wholesale condemnation and developer's dandruff. A large number of religious institutions now share Summit Avenue with the fine residences. The spine of the district is Summit Avenue, and today a tour from the Cathedral through the district and on to the termination of Summit at the Mississippi will display a progression of representative residential architecture spanning a century, from 1856 to the 1950s.

Nineteenth-century architectural revivalism has at times been deplored by architectural historians as a manifestation of poor taste and a lack of confidence in indigenous design. Unquestionably the re-creation of architectural styles of earlier days was a reflection of a search for qualities often lacking in contemporary life, and of the belief that the dignity and cohesiveness of earlier epochs could be infused into the chaotic post-Industrial Revolutionary period through a resurrection of architectural styles. The Romantic Movement of the late eighteenth and the nineteenth centuries is laced with this, and the Middle Ages in particular had a strong hold on nineteenth-century literature, art, and architecture.

Burbank-Livingston-Griggs Mansion, 432 Summit Avenue, St. Paul.

One of the more successful American revivalists was Henry Hobson Richardson, who had returned to the East from his student years in Paris deeply impressed with the French Romanesque style. The power conveyed by rock-faced stone surfaces and massive rounded arches resulted in some highly compelling and some tediously somber nineteenth-century architecture in the United States, for Richardson's imitators were legion and did not always understand his principles. The home of James J. Hill, at 240 Summit Avenue, was designed by Peabody and Stearns of Boston and built between the years 1889 and 1891. A massive red sandstone fortress with numerous dormers, the house is one of the largest on Summit Avenue but resembles many of its neighbors with its porte cochere and exaggeratedly tall chimneys. A two-story art gallery within the house contained one of the outstanding collections of the Barbizon school of paintings in this country. Although it would be hard to find this a comfortable house to live in, the Hill mansion is one of the best examples of Richardsonian Romanesque in the metropolitan area.

The entire Historic Hill District offers a variation on a theme of turrets. Some are shy, modestly blending into the rest of a building, others are brazen strumpets such as the tower marking the corner of Laurel Terrace at Nina Street and Laurel Avenue. At 266 Summit is the Driscoll-Weyerhaeuser house, built in 1884, with a tower thrusting confidently into the air, a reminder in brick of Frederick Weyerhaeuser, captain of the lumber industry!

In 1865 James Burbank, whose wealth derived from the transport business of the Minnesota Stage Company, chose to build his mansion of local limestone in Italianate style at 432 Summit Avenue, at a time when most of his contemporaries were still building in Irvine Park below. Like so many other styles in Minnesota the Italian villa was not a true revival or a copy of an earlier style, but rather an expression of late eighteenth-century English romanticism, largely inspired by the seventeenth-century painters Nicolas Poussin and Claude Lorrain. The neo-sort-of-Italian result in the Twin Cities has a low pitched roof with brackets under extended eaves and, in the case of the Burbank home, round arched windows.

Burbank's architect, Otis Wheelock of Chicago, used two-story polygonal bays and his brackets are particularly elegant with their pendants. The Burbank home has a windowed cupola, a feature frequently topping off the Italianate villa. The home was ahead of its time in being outfitted with steam heat, hot and cold running water, and gas lighting. But what happened to this mansion exemplifies architectural derivativeness in these cities. In the 1920s and 1930s Mary Griggs, a subsequent owner, remodeled every room with the exception of the overly ornate Victorian Gothic hallway. There are an eighteenth-century Venetian dining room with a marble floor and English Sheraton furniture, an eighteenth-century mirror room (whose mirrors are past their prime), a Louis XV sitting room done in delicate good taste, and an art deco recreation room in the basement. The limestone exterior remains handsome in its relative simplicity. Inside, the attempt to re-create Continental luxury in the Middle West misfires but the result is nevertheless an interesting revelation of the aspirations of one wealthy St. Paulite. The house is usually known as the Livingston-Griggs mansion, named for the later owners, Crawford Livingston and his daughter and son-in-law Theodore and Mary Griggs. In 1967 Mrs. Griggs's daughter gave the mansion to the Minnesota Historical Society and it is now open to the public.

During the years 1917 and 1918 novelist Sinclair Lewis lived at 516 Summit Avenue where he worked on his play, *Hobohemia*, based on one of his early "virtue will win" stories. During that year the peripatetic Lewis rented this yellow brick Italian villa with its stone quoins—dressed stones at the corners which give the effect of outlining the house—and romantically round arched windows. Although *Hobohemia* is a eulogy to middle western virtues Lewis was undoubtedly storing up material for his later satirical masterpiece, *Babbitt*.

Many of the grand homes in St. Paul and Minneapolis built in the last three decades of the nineteenth century are in the Queen Anne style, the "anything goes" or bric-a-brac style. A conscious blending of a number of Renaissance and medieval forms and unlike the simple dignified homes of Queen Anne's reign in the early eighteenth century, it was another nineteenth-century expression of romanticism which appeared in the Middle West in the 1870s after its adoption by Norman Shaw and Philip Webb in England. The home designed for Herman Greve at 445 Summit and built in 1884 is one of the best local examples of the Queen Anne style. It is a successful joining of an unlikely combination—limestone, stucco, half-timbering, and shingles—into an ample structure. Ironically, one of the effects striven for in these homes was that of the Elizabethan cottage, though the very people who lived in such homes would probably have been horrified at the notion of building a cottage on Summit Avenue.

For the voluptuary of Victoriana 513 Summit provides a plumcake of picturesque ingredients termed American Queen Anne. The eye boggles before a conically topped tower which counterpoints an elaborately frosted gable punctured by a mixture of window shapes. Below, first- and second-story bay windows leave nothing to the imagination. A homey veranda wraps up this architectural jumble.

The sturdy but stylish square home found in great variety along Summit Avenue took strong root throughout the more fashionable areas of St. Paul and Minneapolis. Cass Gilbert's design at 705 Summit, built for department store executive Jacob Dittenhofer in 1899, is a matronly yellow limestone mansion with three pointed Gothic arches and steeply gabled dormers. Nearby at 804 Lincoln Avenue there is a handsome example of this style with a porte cochere, wrought-iron gate, and vines which soften the limestone. Homes built by wealthy Twin Citians were more conservative than their counterparts in the East, with a few exceptions such as the ostentatious castle built by Swan Turnblad, owner of the largest Swedish-language newspaper in America. This architectural smorgasbord at 2600 Park Avenue in Minneapolis, now the American Swedish Institute, apparently intimidated even the Turnblads, for after a brief residence they moved to an apartment across the street! As one looks at the array of squares on Summit, the thought occurs that they are a reflection of the "feet on the ground" atmosphere which continues to prevail in these cities.

Novelist F. Scott Fitzgerald called Summit Avenue "a museum of architectural failures," but it was, nevertheless, a museum that represented the unattainable to him throughout his early years and has been widely accepted as one of the prime ingredients in his artistic development. His birthplace at 475-481 Laurel Avenue is a drab three-story structure on the periphery of the fashionable district. His family, ever in financial straits, moved frequently and lived for various periods in different homes within the Historic Hill District, on streets such as Holly, which symbolized second-class citizenship to the socially conscious young Fitzgerald. In 1919, "in a house below the average/of a street above the average/in a room below the roof" Fitzgerald wrote much of *This Side of Paradise*, his first successful novel. This is 599 Summit Avenue, part of a series of eight attached dwellings which are an 1889 riot of witch's cap turrets, bay windows, gables, and recessed doorways. Fitzgerald would be amused that Summit Terrace now appears in the National Historic Register and that the once déclassé row house is now considered as charming a dwelling as the more ample homes of the Hills and Weyerhaeusers, and that of his grandmother McQuillan at 629 Summit Avenue.

Summit Terrace, 587-601 Summit Avenue, St. Paul.
F. Scott Fitzgerald lived at Number 599 when he
was writing This Side of Paradise.

At 1006 Summit the state governor's mansion sprawls in Jacobean flamboyance, with high gables and chimneys, dating from 1910. Scattered along the avenue are a number of fine Georgian structures, such as that at 1017 Summit, quietly symmetrical descendents of American colonial homes. In recent years there has been such a rage for the consciously eccentric in Victorian architecture that some of these rather formal, lovely brick and wood homes with dormer windows and small central porticoes are ignored. Fortunately a number of them can be seen in both cities in neighborhoods once inhabited by wealthy citizens.

Here and there along Summit Avenue from Dale Street to the river are homes built in the decades 1910 to 1930, many of them watered down pic-

Robert Halladay

Commodore Hotel bar, art deco in the Historic Hill District, St. Paul. Legend has it that F. Scott Fitzgerald drank here.

Heidi Schwabacher

Residence at 2022 Summit Avenue, St. Paul, a prairie-style house designed by George Elmslie and William Gray Purcell, 1912.

Tudor, Upper Middle West Spanish hacienda, Dutch Colonial cottages—they were the logical progeny of the Queen Anne home of an earlier day. The result is a certain tediousness. The money that went into these homes could have purchased a Frank Lloyd Wright or a Purcell and Elmslie design such as the very handsome Prairie-style home built for Dr. Ward Beebe at 2022 Summit in 1912. Its singular simplicity stands out amongst some undistinguished models of conformity surrounding it. Examples of post-World War II slicked-up ranch-style homes bring Summit to the middle of the twentieth century.

East from Summit, Ramsey Street leads the urban explorer with a sharp and sudden descent into a very different St. Paul. Irvine Park, one of the oldest existing enclaves of homes in Minnesota, is now on the National Historic Register. The park was once the home of nineteenth-century leaders of St. Paul, having preceded Summit Avenue as a choice residential site. Its location between Fort Snelling and downtown St. Paul and its proximity to the then thriving Seven Corners commercial area were particularly strategic. Although the neighborhood has declined, enough remains to be salvaged. And the presence of winding streets with their lovely old trees within sight of downtown St. Paul reinforces the feeling that the city is really a big small town.

In the mid-nineteenth century the mansard or curb roof was used as a sign of elegance in many homes, a style with a vaguely French connection which had developed during the period of the Second Empire. One of the finest local examples and fortunately the one house in Irvine Park which has remained in mint condition is the home of Alexander Ramsey at 265 South Exchange Street.

turesque or "period" houses. After World War I particularly, there was a fad for the supposedly modern home that bears a suspiciously close resemblance to the Victorian villa. Irregular outlines were thought to contribute a picturesque air, verandas have often disappeared, terraces and carports signalize a "modern" air. Frequently these hybrids sport a pointed Gothic entry way, and larger ones a double arched entrance with stucco and woods mixed in varying degrees. Stockbroker's

Robert Halladay

American Swedish Institute, 2600 Park Avenue, Minneapolis.

Ramsey was a governor of Minnesota when it was a territory and later when it was a state. Subsequently he became a United States senator and a secretary of war. Between 1868 and 1872 he built this mansion of local limestone, with the long narrow windows and dormers so frequently found in upper-class Victorian homes. In many ways the Ramsey house typifies the fine nineteenth-century homes of St. Paul and Minneapolis, for it is a more conservative interpretation of a style which made its way westward after being filtered through the vision of eastern Americans. It is a mansion, but its scale is human and it has a comfortable lived-in look with the expectable veranda, ample grounds, and old trees, and it is surrounded by a graceful cast-iron fence. The high-ceilinged rooms are a marvel of Victorian pretension to fashion, consistently missing the mark of true elegance by striving too hard. The furnishings today are based on patterns and furniture known to be in the home in the nineteenth century. Patterned drapes clash with patterned wallpaper, rooms are stuffed with furniture. Unless and until Irvine Park as a whole is restored, it is the Ramsey house and grounds which remain as a testament to upper-middle-class life in a nineteenth-century St. Paul neighborhood. The Ramsey house, now maintained by the Minnesota Historical Society, is open to the public.

Down the street from the Ramsey home is a somewhat more modest mansard-roofed dwelling at 302 Exchange Street, the Holcombe-Averill-Jaggard home. Another aging beauty is a Greek Revival home at 223 Walnut Street, known as the Wright-Prendergast house. Considered one of the best examples of late Greek Revival architecture in the area, it is in particularly heart-rending condition. A filthy dark yellow, it stands at the end of Walnut Street where a huge grain storage terminal cuts out any view of the river and bluffs beyond. The dead and dying cars scattered nearby add to the gloom of what looks like a Tennessee Williams stage set. The first section of the house was built in 1851 and an Ionic portico was added in 1906. Around the corner is the Willis-Irvine home, a modified Charles Addams, with steeply pitched roof and flat-topped turret. Built in 1850 the house is today an amalgam of the cottage of John Irvine and the home of St. Paul lawyer Charles Willis. Irvine, one of St. Paul's original townsite owners, gave to the city the park land for which the neighborhood is named.

Mixed in with the formerly grand homes of Irvine Park are a group covered with the saddest of all twentieth-century building materials, asbestos fake brick. The actual park is a gently rolling piece of land surrounded by the once fine homes. From here, downtown St. Paul is clearly visible and the Cathedral looms in splendor on high.

Nearly buried by bars, liquor stores, and roaring traffic on West Seventh Street nearby is the Justus Ramsey home, one of the oldest houses in the city. It is thought to date from the 1850s and to have been the home of the brother of Governor Alexander Ramsey. Currently it is owned by an antique dealer with a shop next door and sits back from the street in its little jungle of bushes and trees. The Justus Ramsey house is a tiny two-story limestone building with walls two feet thick. A pewter cigar store Indian—Sitting Bull dressed in ceremonial robes for his visit to Washington—guards the old farmhouse. Nearby, the Louise Block, a group of nineteenth-century buildings, is a reminder that this was once a vital commercial area.

Although still largely cities of single-family

Alexander Ramsey House, 265 South Exchange Street, St. Paul, completed in 1872.

Justus Ramsey House, 252 West Seventh Street, St. Paul.

dwellings, St. Paul and Minneapolis have become increasingly multiple-dwelling areas. A recent type of structure which seems to proliferate is the deliberately dowdy, three-story walkup, with an exaggerated mansard roof that ends by looking more like a grass thatched topping which I dub "Tahitian shack" style. Thousands of such units have mushroomed in both cities in the past decade. Unfortunately zoning laws have done little to discourage them. Residents stay a short time and developers apparently like it that way, for short-term tenants are unlikely to join tenants' unions. Of older multiple-dwelling units, the dreary but reliable two-family house of clapboard found throughout the United States gives certain sections of each city an anonymous look.

Townhouses have appeared in both cities. Town Oaks in Southwest Minneapolis has been built in a stable residential neighborhood, but regrettably little care went into the design and a clean, neat army barracks is the result. Somewhat more appealing because of variations in placement and a more imaginative design are the townhouses in the Phillips neighborhood in Minneapolis on the site of the former South High School.

Recently, high-rise dwellings have appeared as

ominous signals on our landscape. Ominous, because they usually lack style and blot out views. Few are as offensive as the walkup shacks, but few do much to make a case for themselves in style or individuality. In the financially plagued new-town-in-town, Cedar-Riverside, just west of the University of Minnesota West Bank campus, an attempt has been made to introduce diversity in a cluster of buildings of differing heights. Brightly colored inserts have been placed on the gray concrete exteriors, but on the whole the effect is rather that of makeup on a hopelessly ugly creature.

More encouraging is the sudden interest in renovating older row houses, especially in the Historic Hill District of St. Paul where a number were in salvageable condition and where the neighborhoods generally had not deteriorated or succumbed to freeways. The truly successful ones, such as those on Holly Avenue, are owner-occupied dwellings, where tender loving care has set an example for living on an increasingly crowded planet.

Twin Citians are fond of showing visitors through the lake areas of Minneapolis, driving them along the winding, seductive Minnehaha Parkway where park lawns slope down to the creek. St. Paul's Summit Avenue and Como Park and the river roads of both cities are used to demonstrate a success story, apparently one without slums. Statistics of the ratio of park land to residents sound impressive. But the picture is distorted if presented in this way. There is no concentration of slums, but there is a flatness about the look of many neighborhoods and parks are not always provided to relieve the blandness. It is the flatness of boiled potatoes and stale gingerale, of a feeling that something could have been done to enliven the homes and surroundings built for people with little money. Both cities grew rapidly and a dismal lack of imagination in planning for middle- and lower-middle-class residential areas is evident. Some Twin Citians put a great deal of care into these modest homes, and it must be admitted that ugly ducklings are not necessarily neglected. But you can drive and walk through block after block in either city feeling a mild despair over the look of residential areas.

The neighborhoods of Northeast Minneapolis near the river—St. Anthony, Holland, and Sheridan—disprove the picture of the cities as being made up of families able to hop into a canoe in the front yard, cross the street to tee off for golf on weekend afternoons, or turn the children loose in the park next door. This area has shockingly little park and playground space. Railroads and industry early made incursions.

These neighborhoods sum up much of the undistinguished middle way, so characteristic of the Twin Cities. Topographical flatness is reinforced by architectural insipidity. A number of large two-family homes built in the early years of the century in neutral stucco, faceless fourplexes, and architecturally uninteresting smaller homes contribute to the stereotypical conception of a middle western city, a stereotype that is too frequently borne out in Minneapolis and St. Paul. The plethora of chain link fences does little to enhance aesthetics. In the late nineteenth century the Minneapolis Brewing and Malting Company (later the Grain Belt Brewery) threw up a schmaltzy Rhine castle brewery at 1215 Northeast Marshall Street and subsequently a garden oasis with a mini-geyser, a deer park, and well-landscaped grounds to embellish it. Within recent years the handsome white brick Webster Intermediate School on Fifth Street Northeast has given a lift to its area. But little else has been done to soften the general insult that commerce and industry have offered to these family-centered neighborhoods.

Yet the drawing power is there. In an area in St. Anthony bounded by Northeast Fifth and Seventh avenues, Main and Marshall streets, decaying homes were torn down after the Housing and Redevelopment Authority acquired the land in the 1960s. Lots for new homes were sold and residents who have deep roots in this section of the city have built or bought large expensive homes in spite of the presence of depressing industrial blight and traffic on Marshall Street. The pull of old neighborhood ties, of church and club membership, is strong enough to commit these residents to homes very similar in price and style to those in affluent suburbs. More modest homes have been built throughout these neighborhoods within recent years, a notable number on the "presidential" streets such as Monroe, Madison, and Quincy.

Other signs of strong faith in the future of these neighborhoods can be seen in time donated by residents for face-lifting measures. In the mid-seventies a junkyard at the conjunction of Summer Street and Central Avenue was converted by residents into a playground, vegetable garden, and grassed-in park space. But they are still saddled with the roar of traffic and the gasoline fumes from two truck routes, Central Avenue and Broadway Northeast, all presided over by a Land-O-Nod mattress sign!

Throughout Minneapolis and St. Paul one of the most telling visual expressions of the ethnic mix is the church architecture, for many of these buildings were conscious imitations of churches attended in the homeland. Sometimes a particular church was duplicated and sometimes the availability of different building materials and other considerations led to changes in design, but there is no question that the tie to a native land was more often reflected in ecclesiastical architecture than in residential or mercantile buildings. And this is not surprising. The church was the focal point for social as well as religious life for newly arrived immigrants, providing the gathering place of a ready-made group who spoke the same language and could offer a buffer against a frightening and confusing new environment. This is particularly evident in Northeast Minneapolis, where church buildings tell us much of the immigration patterns during the nineteenth and twentieth centuries, and where neighborhood ties and church attendance are still strong. There is a high proportion of churches to residents, including a large number of Catholic churches of the Eastern rite.

The undulating roofline of St. Constantine's Ukrainian Catholic Church at the corner of Fifth Street and University Avenue Northeast, built in the 1970s, features an exotic oriental blue, gold, and red dome in strong contrast to the mundane character of the homes here. The horizontality of this large church is noteworthy when we look at St. Mary's Russian Orthodox Greek Catholic Church at 1701 Fifth Street Northeast, the pièce de résistance in this section of the city. It is a tall building whose green copper dome and exciting onion-shaped spire create a strange tension. The distinctive Russian cross with an angled crossbar near its base is repeated a number of times on the building. As you walk around it the huge green copper dome and the smaller onion-shaped turrets overlap in a variety of geometric configurations, while the long round-arched windows have an air of mystery and power.

Within the church the iconostasis presents a particularly rich and strange combination of Byzantine painted figures and Western influences such as are seen in the Berniniesque twisted columns similar to those in St. Peter's.

Since St. Mary's is part of the Russian branch of the Greek Orthodox Church the building, completed in 1905, was paid for by the czar for the congregation of Russian-speaking émigrés from the Carpathian Mountains. These immigrants had begun to settle in this area in the 1870s and 80s to work in the factories and nearby sawmills.

It is appropriate that the Pioneer's Square Monument, a WPA-style granite tribute to three generations, was moved from the downtown post office grounds to St. Anthony West in 1967. As a work of art it leaves something to be desired, but it deserves its place in one of the oldest sections of what is now Minneapolis and one that has welcomed successive waves of immigrants. This section of Northeast Minneapolis began as the town of St. Anthony in 1850, expanding northward as the lumber mills grew along the Mississippi. The earliest settlers were Swedes, Norwegians, Germans, and Poles. Later Czechs, Slovaks, and Ukrainians arrived as earlier settlers moved to other parts of the city. A Scandinavian legacy remains in the late-nineteenth-century Emanuel Evangelical Lutheran Church at Monroe Street and Thirteenth Avenue Northeast. Most of the parishioners have now moved to other sections of the Twin Cities although they return to attend services in this distinctively northern European, neo-Gothic building.

Other churches such as St. Michael's Ukrainian at Fifth Avenue and Fourth Street and St. John's

St. Mary's Russian Orthodox Greek Catholic Church, 1701 Northeast Fifth Street, Minneapolis.

49

Byzantine Catholic Church at Twenty-second Avenue and Third Street attest to the heavy concentration of people of Eastern European descent in Northeast. Church pastors, insurance agents, and funeral directors bear Polish, Czech, Ukrainian, and Slovak names. But there is in addition a Lebanese group in St. Anthony, many of them forming the congregation of St. Maron at 602 University Avenue Northeast.

That there is still much consciousness of the residents' ethnic heritage can be seen in such organizations as the Ukrainian Congress Committee, the Ukrainian Home Society, and the Ukrainian Credit Union, all housed in the building at 28 Northeast Second Street. The Ukrainian Congress Committee is the Minnesota branch of a national cultural institution, dedicated to fostering awareness of their heritage among Ukrainian immigrants and their descendants. It sponsors, among other things, dances and concerts, and selects textbooks on Ukrainian life which are used in local parochial schools. Throughout Northeast, ethnic bakeries, Polish-power bumper stickers, a Lebanese delicatessen, and a Ukrainian gift shop add to the mix. Neighborhood bars are like English pubs where the regulars know one another and frequent them to socialize rather than to drink in solitary gloom.

At the juncture of Kenwood Parkway and West Lake of the Isles Boulevard is a stone marker bearing a plaque with the following inscription: "Peavey Fountain. Given to the people of Minneapolis in 1891 by F. H. Peavey as a drinking fountain for horses. This monument was rededicated as a memorial to the horses of the 151st Field Artillery, Minnesota National Guard, killed in action in the First World War, 1917-1918." Originally a watering trough and now a flower container, this whimsical memorial is not out of place in the Kenwood neighborhood, for if there is a horsey set in the Twin Cities, a good representation resides in this section of Minneapolis. Some few decades ago a bridal path around Lake of the Isles made possible the aristocratic sport, and the lake district as a whole is still a paradise for walking, boating, and swimming in summer. Cold weather brings out skaters and cross-country skiers, and throughout the region there is more than ample room on the gentle slopes for sledding. The parkways, verdant in spring and summer, thread their labyrinthine way around Lake of the Isles and Lakes Calhoun, Harriet, Nokomis, and Hiawatha, and Diamond Lake.

The luxuriously landscaped Lake of the Isles, with its plethora of conifers and deciduous trees, is one of the most romantic spots in either Minneapolis or St. Paul. The Italianate palazzi, Spanish casas, American neo-Georgian, and French provincial style residences which cram the boulevard are architectural counterparts of the romantically landscaped lake. These very large residences are like socially ambitious matrons crowding one another for the best view of the most beautiful city lake.

As Minneapolis's answer to the most elegant sections of the Historic Hill District in St. Paul, the Kenwood and Lowry Hill neighborhoods are rich in the records of this city's upper-class residences. The mansions here are noticeably younger than those on the older section of Summit as the area was built up largely from the 1890s. Those homes constructed in recent decades were often built on the grounds of earlier, larger mansions. At 1650

Dupont South is the house designed and built for the late sculptor John Rood by Elizabeth and Winston Close in 1949. This beautiful structure of gray shake and Mendota limestone incorporates the retaining walls and gateposts of a nineteenth-century mansion which stood on these grounds. At 1700 Mount Curve Avenue the residence designed by architect Robert Bliss was designated by *Architectural Record* one of the twenty finest American homes built in 1964. Characteristically, it is on the property of the early-twentieth-century estate of the Donaldson family, whose department store is on Nicollet Mall. E. E. Atkinson, whose beswagged mansion stands at the corner of Logan and Lincoln avenues, founded an early Minneapolis department store. A stucco Italian Renaissance palazzo at 1711 Emerson was built in 1926 for another Nicollet Avenue proprietor, Elizabeth Quinlan. These merchandisers were so close to town and on high enough ground that they could almost literally oversee the premises of their emporiums.

Gone is the five-acre estate of streetcar magnate Thomas Lowry who developed Lowry Hill with his father-in-law, Calvin Goodrich. The land is now occupied by the Walker Art Center, The Guthrie Theater, and an insurance company. And gone are the streetcars, but an enduring legacy of Lowry remains in this and other neighborhoods which grew up as the streetcar lines extended south and west. The growth of the lake district as a residential area took place after 1892 when the electric streetcar was introduced although the regions farthest south and west grew after World War I.

The lake district embraces a very wide range of homes and although the five-room bungalow was seldom built quite as close to the water as the thirty-room mansion, there are a surprising number of modest homes with easy accessibility to the lakes. Few structures are as interesting architecturally as that designed by Frank Lloyd Wright at 2815 Burnham Boulevard or the home which William Gray Purcell built for himself at 2328 Lake Place, but the neighborhoods are superbly endowed with park land and water and the accompanying opportunities for recreation. Most of it is available for any resident, since, with the exception of the land occupied by the Calhoun Beach Hotel and the exclusive Minikahda Club on Lake Calhoun, the land was early set aside for public use. On a bluff overlooking Lake Calhoun is St. Mary's Greek Orthodox Church, built in 1958. This handsome reminder of Byzantium, with its fine golden dome, may seem a bit out of place in Middle America, but it is one more proof of the ethnically interesting mix of these cities.

Southwest Minneapolis has the largest proportion of developed park areas in the city and unquestionably some of the most satisfactory neighborhoods aesthetically. A very large number of residents live in well-maintained single-unit dwellings. Homes dating from the late nineteenth century can be found, but the largest developments in Southwest took place beginning with the boom period of the 1920s.

Minnehaha Creek must be high on the list of Minneapolis's Chamber of Commerce as a bait to lure potential Minneapolitans, for this half-wild charmer is bounded by neighborhoods that offer the city dweller a place to live in a parklike setting not far from the center of the city. Tangletown (also known as Washburn Park), an enclave of winding streets around the Washburn Tower, is an ever-so-American community of picturesque, 1920s homes. Because of the steep terrain it is al-

Gemma Rossini Cullen

Washburn Water Tower in Tangletown (Washburn Park), Southwest Minneapolis.

ways an attractive neighborhood, but the combination of quiet secluded streets and a tropical growth of trees and bushes in the summer offer all that a resident could want for an inner city neighborhood. The repetitiveness of the architecture is somewhat mitigated by the winding streets. The old water tower was designed by Harry Jones, who let his nostalgia-seeking imagination loose in a striking rounded tower embellished with stark eagles at its top and at the base a group of medieval knights closely resembling the portal figures of Gothic cathedrals. But whereas the homes in the neighborhood are architecturally rehashes of rehashes—Dutch Colonial, Minnesota Spanish, reworking of the Victorian Gothic in the 1920s—Jones's water tower has a more compelling simplicity.

Not far from Tangletown is the Washburn Community Library, named for a family prominent in the milling industry in the nineteenth century. The architectural theme of the building employs a nineteenth-century millstone inside an atrium and an abstract grain pattern in the upper wall of the atrium. Architect Brooks Cavin echoed the circularity of the millstone with an inviting seat around the atrium tree. But the most successful element of the library is its use of borrowed scenery where the lush growth adjoining Minnehaha Creek can be seen through glass walls along the north side of the building. Indeed, on a spring or summer day a romantic reader of any age must leave this handsome building for the even more compelling call of the creek outside.

Not only does the creek run through the Southwest community, but within its boundaries is Lake Harriet with its wooded shoreline and Lyndale Park, which contains the Lake Harriet Rose Gardens. The park is a dolled-up star, with two lovely fountains and the rather formal gardens, but nearby is a wildlife sanctuary. In summer, sailboats perform a continual dance on the lake. A few sections of shoreline are blighted with ugly apartment houses, and too many cars are allowed to park in some areas, but there are stretches of large handsome homes dressed in beautiful green lawns and breathtaking trees. This area closely resembles that of the somewhat more crowded but equally large residences on Lake of the Isles. This is it: the beautiful home with a sailboated lake and the IDS Tower in the distance.

Framed by the Mississippi on the east, by the Milwaukee Railroad marshaling yards on the west, the Franklin Avenue commercial strip on the north, and an industrial park on the south, Seward neighborhood in southern Minneapolis exemplifies the American Drab quality of the cities as contrasted with the dramatic beauty of the river gorge. Small single-unit homes and the 1920s duplexes of wood frame or stucco line streets laid out in the monotonous grid plan, usually bearing anonymous, numbered names. In short, it is not your inner city, townhouse neighborhood, soon to be rediscovered by the flight from suburbia. But it is a representative city neighborhood—railroad tracks, river, industrial park, and modest homes. And it is clearly a livable one.

On November 7, 1884, what later became Milwaukee Avenue in Seward was officially opened as Twenty-second and a Half Avenue, and a more symbolic title could not have been chosen—a numbered street, and not even a whole number, it was a

Robert N. Taylor

Lake Calhoun, Minneapolis.

strip of repetitive houses, thrown up on the smallest possible lots by one of the speculative construction firms interested in squeezing as much money as possible from home owners or renters. The street is an unusually narrow one in a metropolitan area endowed with many generously built boulevards and streets. In 1906 its name was changed to Milwaukee Avenue although it was usually called Copenhagen Avenue because of the large number of Scandinavians living there. Built for working-class immigrants, Milwaukee became the bottom rung on the residential ladder, a place to live in until the worker could afford a better neighborhood. The 1895 census shows that homes were populated by Norwegians, Danes, and Swedes, usually housing five or six people from one family and often taking in a boarder. Looking at the size of the houses and the density of buildings, we can all too clearly imagine the rackety life packed into these two blocks.

Robert Halladay

Fountain in Lyndale Park, Minneapolis.

Eventually Milwaukee Avenue became as unbuttoned as much of the Seward West neighborhood, and by the summer of 1974 many houses had been abandoned, giving a boarded-up ghost town look to the area. But at that time Milwaukee Avenue was placed on the National Historic Register as a monument to working-class life in the late nineteenth and early twentieth centuries.

It is no accident that these two blocks were salvaged for posterity, for the Seward West residents who worked so hard to bring them to the attention of the National Historic Register are representative of a spirit in the neighborhood that has virtually rescued a community from condemnation. When the Minneapolis Housing Authority announced plans to buy up and level sixty percent of Seward West in the early 1960s, a group of residents persuaded it to rehabilitate whatever was salvageable. A Project Area Committee made up of residents saw that rebuilding meant escalating housing costs beyond the pockets of the working-class residents; to prevent this it convinced the Housing Authority to attempt several methods of rehabilitation. Homes marked for destruction are put on the market, largely for the value of the land, on the condition that the purchaser will meet the rehabilitation costs. In addition, a nonprofit corporation, Seward Redesign, buys up as many of the houses as it can afford at one time, rehabilitates them, and then sells them to a preselected group of buyers, with Seward residents having first choice. In other cases, current owners have renovated their own homes. In addition a Minneapolis homesteading arrangement (which applies to any neighborhood in the city) has further extended the Seward West face-lifting. Homes can be bought for $1.00 provided that the new owner will agree to bring the property up to code within a specified period of time. What is unusual about the turnaround in Seward West is that the neighborhood has taken charge of the project and has used innovative methods to revitalize itself.

Driving and walking through the neighborhood give the visitor a lift, for although the asbestos-clad waifs marked for rehabilitation look a bit unpromising, the visitor need only drive to Twenty-fourth Avenue to find a shingled cottage, one of Seward Redesign's successes. Scattered in amongst some uninhabited and other rundown houses are tidy little homes dating from the early years of the community. Here and there are new homes, a sign of confidence in the future of the neighborhood. At the unprepossessing address of Twenty-third Avenue and Twenty-fourth Street are several townhouses in an appealing shingle style, far more attractive than the shack-style three-story walkups built by speculators throughout the cities in the past two decades and an improvement upon the unfortunate dun-colored multiple-dwelling stucco concrete blocks of earlier years.

Seward West has always been a working-class neighborhood made up of small homes on narrow lots, many of them built during the 1880s and 1890s when the city was in its most rapid period of expansion. It was the proximity of railroad yards and factories that attracted workers to these homes when even the expense of a horse-drawn trolley had to be calculated into a weekly budget. A large section of the southern area of Seward was condemned and demolished by the Minneapolis Housing Authority in the 1960s in order to build an industrial park. On the whole the park is an amiable neighbor to the residential area with ample space between the landscaped, low-lying buildings. The

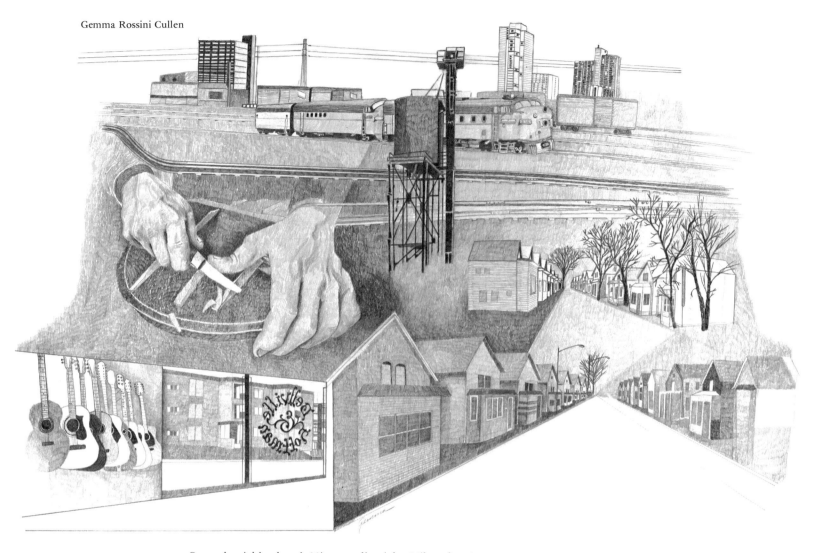

Gemma Rossini Cullen

Seward neighborhood, Minneapolis; right, Milwaukee Avenue.

industry housed in Seward South is typically light industry, ranging from printing and binding firms to the Yum-Yum Noodle Factory.

As the walker moves closer to the river into Seward East the neighborhood shades into a somewhat more affluent area, one very representative of the middle-classness of the Twin Cities. Here too,

many homes are small and close together. The grid plan is relieved by the wayward curve of streets such as Minneapolis Avenue—it is almost as if the street surveyors had imbibed some of the air of freedom from the nearby strong brown god of a river and its wildly tangled banks, for some streets inexplicably break out of the rigid checkerboard.

Seabury Avenue paralleling River Road West continues the architecturally undistinguished stucco beigeness found throughout much of the cities, but its front yard is a beautiful greensward leading to wooded banks and the river itself. The homes become more prosperous looking on the southern rim of the neighborhood—strangely just before the natural beauty is interrupted by a railroad bridge!

Seward is a blatant example of the inequities of park distribution in both cities. Except for paths at the top of the riverbanks—the banks themselves being too steep for anyone except the hardiest climbers to use—very little park land was provided within the neighborhood. The residents petitioned the park and school boards to acquire land on adjacent blocks when the Seward Elementary School was slated for demolition and rebuilding in the 1960s. The result is the Matthews Agency, one of the first park-school-social agencies in the state of Minnesota, whose sharing avoids wasteful duplication of services. Although neither the park nor the buildings are remarkable in design, the neighborhood has clearly gained much in usable open spaces and multiple-service buildings.

That Minneapolis and St. Paul are not populated entirely by middle-class tenders of manicured lawns and gardens and that the cities are not made up of pockets of homogeneous neighborhoods can be seen in the Riverside community of Minneapolis. Adjoining Seward neighborhood, it is one of the oldest in the city and has had one of the more turbulent and varied histories in either city. In the nineteenth and early twentieth centuries it attracted working-class immigrants of various nationalities. In Ole Rölvaag's novel *The Boat of Longing* the protagonist Nils is a young Norwegian living on Cedar Avenue in a boardinghouse appropriately named "Babel." In it Scandinavians, Germans, and Russian Poles find themselves in a rich and sometimes clashing national mix. Respectable working-class families, a disreputable poet, and two young ladies whose occupation requires irregular hours live in "Babel." On a lonely Sunday Nils wanders to the river nearby to find a settlement called Bohemian Flats which is populated by his own countrymen as well as Eastern Europeans.

Nils works as a janitor for several neighborhood saloons. Throughout the area music halls and saloons attracted Scandinavians from all parts of the cities to see the thriving Swedish vaudeville. A vital people's theater, it was a mixture of song and dance and skits about immigrant life. On Washington Avenue at Seven Corners a theater building, now renovated to house Guthrie 2, an experimental theater, pulsed with this vaudeville. Dania Hall on Cedar Avenue with its Gothic tower is one of the few other remaining landmarks of the early days of the Riverside community, for, more than in most city neighborhoods, significant buildings were razed in the decades of decay before the 1960s.

At the corner of Fourth Street and Cedar Avenue stands a minuscule flatiron building, the Triangle Bar, a holdover from the days when Greeks and Ukrainians from the Northside held circle dances on the second-story dance floor. A descendant of the Swedish music halls, today it is a magnet throbbing with the fastest music and so packed on weekend nights that an oxygen mask is said to be required by some customers. The Triangle is a fitting symbol of the clashing mixture which has characterized the community from its earliest days.

Robert Halladay

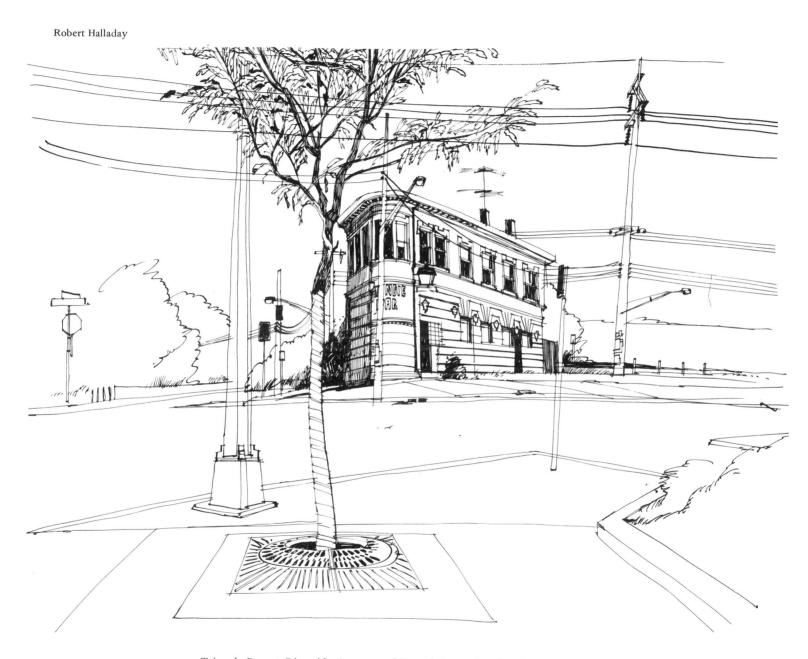

Triangle Bar, at Riverside Avenue and Fourth Street South, Minneapolis.

Gemma Rossini Cullen

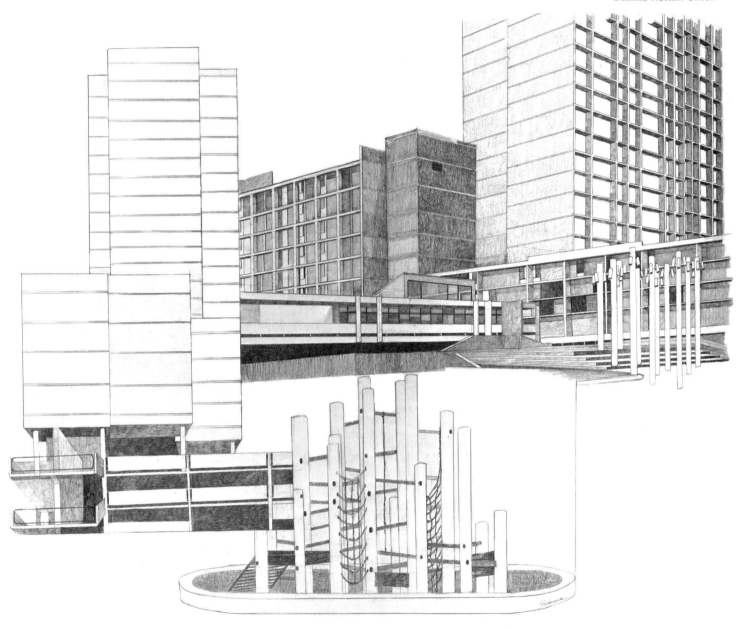

Cedar Riverside New Town-in-Town, Fifth Street South and Cedar Avenue, Minneapolis. Bottom, playground in Stage One of Cedar Riverside.

Riverside has an unusually high proportion of institutions, with two large hospitals, Augsburg College, and the West Bank campus of the University of Minnesota taking up large tracts of land today. The early settlers and their descendants had been leaving the neighborhood for some decades as Riverside followed the pattern of too many inner-city neighborhoods, with neglected property and an influx of criminal elements. Yet a number of older residents remained and in the 1960s university students with long hair and relaxed living habits posed an apparent threat to the remaining stability of the community.

Cedar-Riverside, bounded by Fifth Street South and Cedar Avenue, is this country's first federally designated "new-town-in-town," originally slated to include everything a community would need. Buildings of varying heights were to house 30,000 residents and plans were drawn up to encourage recreational, institutional, and commercial establishments within walking distance. The new-town-in-town received government assistance in the form of a $24-million guarantee of private bonds with the provision that half of the units would also receive some sort of government subsidy to permit people of low and moderate income to live there. During the sixties the developers, Cedar Riverside Associates, bought up much of the residential property, but a large group of residents oppose the Riverside community's being further turned into a high-rise haven. An old neighborhood of small houses was being decimated to make way for a densely populated residential area. Furthermore provisions for development of open spaces fell far short of early plans. Tenant strikes, a class-action suit, and financial difficulties halted the expansion of the Cedar-Riverside new-town-in-town after the completion of Stage One.

Today a sociologist would be hard put to peg the mixture of anonymous high-rise apartment buildings, older buildings electrically alive with supergraphics, crafts shops, bars, coffee houses, bookstores, and the remaining out-at-the-elbow small frame houses with their lilac bushes, vegetable gardens, and picket fences. It is a most unlikely patchwork quilt made up of Greenwich Village, Gopher Prairie, and Brasilia.

St. Anthony Park in St. Paul might be the last selected as a typical Twin Cities neighborhood since it is somewhat cut off from the rest of the city, is actually much closer to downtown Minneapolis than downtown St. Paul, has relatively few grid-plan streets, and has a number of sprawling old homes instead of middle western boxes. Yet that peculiar conjunction of small town/big city, of old/new, of being an oasis is highlighted in this community of approximately 5,500 residents. A desert of ugly railroad tracks cuts it off from South St. Anthony Park, on the west Highway 280 provides a constant aural reminder of our automotive desecration, and the campus of the University of Minnesota runs a barrier on the east. But the isolation is not really a misfortune, for St. Anthony Park is more like a village than most neighborhoods of any city. At its center, where Carter-Como-Doswell avenues meet, are a post office, a bank, a library, a grocery, a drugstore, a bookstore, a restaurant, and a gas station. It is main street. The half-timbered Tudorbethan buildings housing several commercial establishments in Milton Square, and the nicely proportioned Italian Renaissance library built in 1917 are charming remnants of the eclectic era.

One of a number of residential parks laid out in St. Paul and Minneapolis in the nineteenth century, St. Anthony Park was originally intended to be an exclusive suburb of large country estates. William Marshall, governor of Minnesota from 1866 to 1870, began to buy up land in the area as early as the 1850s. In the 1870s others joined him in his speculative venture, including his brother-in-law Nicholas Langford (who later became the first superintendent of Yellowstone Park) and John Knapp, president of a Wisconsin lumber company. In 1873 Marshall engaged Horace Cleveland to design a residential suburb and though the park has changed considerably, Cleveland's insistence on preserving as much as possible of the natural beauty of the landscape has given St. Anthony Park a highly individual and appealing physiognomy, with gracefully curving streets which discourage speeding and encourage leisurely rambles. The trees in the park are some of the most beautiful in either city and will remain so if the strenuous efforts at preservation and replanting now underway are continued.

The architectural mix adds to the pleasure of the topographical variety, as homes were built from the late nineteenth century to the 1960s. Nor are they all of a size although there are a number of large, Victorian, single-family dwellings that strike a nostalgic chord in us whether we actually grew up in such homes or not. At 2203 and 2205 Scudder are two turreted old lovelies, the former once the home of Governor Andrew McGill. The home at 2107 Commonwealth Avenue was once the St. Anthony depot, built in the 1870s and later bought and moved to this location. The porch was the passenger shelter. Throughout the park comfortable verandas, bay windows, and almost smugly spacious homes are reminders of bygone waste-space days, yet this is not a neighborhood of great wealth. The spectrum is from quite modest wooden or stucco dwellings to the larger homes, but the feeling is that of a comfortable middle-classness.

On Doswell Avenue, a red tree house beckons the nostalgic and at the corner of Raymond and Buford a white clapboard home has a stable turned garage. Bordered by Carter, Doswell, and Raymond avenues is College Park, every child's dream of the perfect sledding park. Formed of a gentle gully, it has trees enough for beauty, yet open space galore

Gemma Rossini Cullen

St. Anthony Park, St. Paul. Lower right, home built in 1889 at 2203 Scudder Street,
originally that of Governor Andrew McGill.

63

to glide on in winter. Where Hythe Street curves away from College Park, on a beautiful sunny winter's day, one could be looking at any middle-class American suburb, the suburban middle-class-ness so maligned and satirized in recent decades. Yet the quiet livableness of this neighborhood is seductive. Even the St. Anthony cooperative grocery store at Buford and Cleveland avenues—although dedicated to stocking the same whole-grain and fresh foods as other coops in the cities—is middle-class clean and staffed by noncounterculture types.

An unusually large proportion of heads of households here have advanced degrees or have studied beyond their bachelor's degrees. The park is within walking distance of the University of Minnesota's St. Paul campus and not far from the university's campus in Minneapolis, and it has its complement of professors, but it also seems to attract a wide variety of well-educated residents who work in various professions in both cities, undoubtedly drawn by the presence of like-minded neighbors.

At the corner of Scudder Street and Como Avenue is a tiny open-air fresh vegetable and flower market which spreads itself out upon stone walls in good weather. The proprietor leaves explicit instructions to the customer that "this is a self-service market, please leave EXACT CHANGE or a check for all purchases." The trust implicit in a self-service market is indicative of a spirit in the park. The neighborhood has had a long history of concerned citizenship which began well before the recent upsurge in community awareness. The St. Anthony Park Improvement Association, formed in 1910, early recognized the need for community planning. A St. Anthony Park Historical Society was founded in 1944 and a few years later became the Ramsey County Historical Society. Presently an active neighborhood association is coming to grips with threats to the residential character of the neighborhood, although it is felt that pressures from commerce and the university may be overwhelming. There is a transient population consisting of students who live in fraternity and boarding-houses. The campus itself is a lovely annex to the neighborhood; its hilly topograpy and the amount of open space give it an air of a country campus, quite different from that of its sibling in Minneapolis. Commonwealth Terrace, university-owned housing for students, carries out the spirit of the park, for it is a cooperative housing project in which tenants do most of the work. But potential university expansion, a transient population, and the daily traffic into the area connected with the university have made inroads upon this village within the city.

In 1964 the neighborhood churches sponsored a town meeting to awaken the residents to the problems which threatened to change this seemingly halcyon life. Under the guidance of Frederic Steinhauser, an urban geographer from the university, ninety-seven percent of the dwelling units were visited. Recommendations for land use, for zoning, for improving parks and playgrounds were made. Homeowners were urged to renovate dwellings badly in need of repair, and landscape architects made a survey of trees with recommendations for reforestation, particularly since the park has a very large number of elms. Proposals for extensive improvements to Langford and College parks were presented to the St. Paul City Council and subsequently carried out. Further evidence of the impact of this neighborhood group is that in the late 1960s St. Anthony Park led the way to the form-

ROBERT N. TAYLOR

Gibbs Farm Museum, 2097 Larpenteur Avenue West, St. Paul, built by Heman Gibbs in the 1850s and 1860s.
On the grounds is the Old Stoen School, a one-room schoolhouse built in 1878 and
moved here from Chippewa County. Other buildings contain a rich assortment
of nineteenth-century tools, carriages, buggies, and sleighs.

ing of the Association of St. Paul Communities, made up of twenty-four neighborhood councils.

Although the park is not rich in playground space the Luther Theological campus on the west and the university's on the east add immeasurably to the feeling of well-being. It is a border community, buffered from suburban development by the experimental agricultural fields of the university on the north. Driving north on Cleveland Avenue past the university you are very quickly in open fields, and at the corner of Larpenteur and Cleveland stands the Gibbs Farm Museum, a mid-nineteenth-century farmhouse maintained by the Ramsey County Historical Society. It is a reminder of the accessibility of rural life to city dwellers, for the county now rents plots of land on the farm to anyone who wishes to raise his own food.

The Dale-Thomas community in St. Paul was given the nickname Frogtown in the nineteenth century, possibly because of the number of swamps nearby. It is a neighborhood of small homes, some of them crowded onto lots thirty feet wide, and many of the homes have been handed down from one generation to another within the same family. A plain Jane neighborhood, woefully deficient in parks, it would never win a City Beautiful Contest, but it is distinguished by one building, the magnificent baroque Church of St. Agnes.

The parish of St. Agnes was founded in 1887 when the Great Northern Railroad built the Dale Street Shops and roundhouse. Many members of the Assumption parish in downtown St. Paul were railroad workers and necessarily moved to be near their jobs. The parishioners were immigrants from the Austro-Hungarian Empire and at least seventeen different ethnic groups made up the parish which was tied together largely by the German language. The incongruously dramatic church, built by nickles and dimes, was an expression of homesickness for their native lands, pride in their community, and deep religious devotion. Unquestionably, it was also proof of the failure of the melting pot, for the years during which it was being erected, 1900-1912, saw an intensification of anti-German feeling and the growing sea of hostility around them undoubtedly drove the parishioners to erect this church building of great splendor. For the parishioners of St. Agnes this hostility reached a crescendo when a bomb exploded in the rectory in 1917.

Normally the tower would have been placed at the front of the church, but during the years of construction a trolley car line was built along Thomas Avenue, making it dangerous for the congregation to enter on that street. The fine entrance, now on Lafond Avenue, is typical of European baroque churches built in the seventeenth and eighteenth centuries as a manifestation of the church triumphant during the Counter-Reformation. A grand flight of steps, a rounded balustrade, and an imposing façade are impressive. But it is the tower at the back that startles the walker in Frogtown, for rising two hundred and five feet above the pavement is an onion-shaped tower one would expect to come upon in southern Germany or Austria. Movement is the key word for the effect achieved by the windows, cupola, and bell tower apertures. It is a classic example of the derivative nature of Twin Cities architecture, but it is also a fine demonstration of what a group of poor people built when driven in on themselves and dedicated to a faith.

Gemma Rossini Cullen

Frogtown (Dale-Thomas neighborhood), St. Paul. Center, three views of St. Agnes Church.

Robert N. Taylor

Mattocks School, on the Highland Park Junior-Senior High School campus, St. Paul, built in 1871 and moved here in the 1960s.

St. Agnes parochial school, far from floundering and closing like so many Catholic schools, has increasing numbers of children. It is said that people still move here to send their children to both the elementary and high schools, and it is certain that families who have lived here for generations continue to send their children to St. Agnes.

Robert N. Taylor

At the conjunction of Montreal and Snelling avenues in St. Paul is the campus of Highland Park Junior and Senior High schools, an ample summation of the good life. The newest of St. Paul's residential areas, Highland Park has grown up largely since the end of World War II and could easily be mistaken for a suburb by anyone not familiar with city boundary lines. The school buildings themselves, designed by Hammel Green Associates and built in the 1950s, are handsome contemporary public structures. The pale beige brick is accented by vertical strips of dark metal with a brilliant but subtle focal point in a low-lying vermilion central building. Across Snelling Avenue stretches Highland Park itself, a visual treat with the river bluffs beyond.

On the school grounds is the one-room Mattocks schoolhouse built in 1871 and moved here during the 1960s. It is a charming building of local gray limestone with walls twenty inches thick and a bell tower—a fitting reminder of the rugged simplicity of life in a smaller St. Paul, and a nostalgic statement in conjunction with the sleekness of the newer school buildings.

At the other end of Highland Park along the Mississippi River Boulevard is the Temple of Aaron, a synagogue designed by Percival Goodman and built in the 1950s. An interesting tension is created between the three symmetrical pointed arches and the ample landscaping. The interior makes use of the abstract designs in stained-glass windows of brilliant orange-red-yellow hue and subdued wood and brick.

On the eastern edge of the community the mid-twentieth century's answer to such highstepping boulevards as Summit Avenue is Edgcumbe Road, winding on the ridge of a hill, with houses ranging from pillared Mount Vernon suburban manses to sprawlingly lovely fieldstone contemporary. The landscaping on Edgcumbe and nearby streets is as beautiful as any to be found in St. Paul or Minneapolis. The terrain, already endowed with hills and views of the bluffs on the opposite side of the river, has been imaginatively embellished with a wide variety of coniferous and deciduous trees along the boulevard. These, in turn, are augmented by the finely landscaped residential property. As a practical matter the variety of planting is more realistic than the stately but vulnerable elm-lined streets of earlier days.

Not all of the Highland Park community boasts such imaginative planning and certain sections are grid-planned with dull homes. The shopping center, Highland Village, is a *Better Homes and Gardens* suburban nonentity, and nearby the Ford Assembly Plant eats up an enormous acreage along the Mississippi Boulevard. And because the park is so uniformly well fed there is a certain boredom in driving through it. It makes you want to locate just one rundown home, just one garden wrecker or crabgrass specialist. But Highland Park presents the culmination of the American residential dream, a garden suburb with the amenities of two city centers close by.

The West Side of St. Paul is not really on the west side in relation to downtown St. Paul but on the south side of the Mississippi. Repeated efforts to rename it Riverview have failed to make any inroads on this rather unusual area. Speculation on the provenance of the confusing name has suggested that riverboat pilots referred to the east or west side of the river throughout its length and resolutely called this portion of St. Paul the West Side. In 1973 when a community newspaper was inaugurated it irrationally but understandably came out as *The West Side Voice*. And a community voice it is indeed. School and community sports are covered, but fundamental issues such as crime prevention, availability of home rehabilitation loans, and the excitement caused by the Spanish-English bilingual program in the public schools are included, and neighborhood personalities are featured. The mix of cultures within the community is apparent in these twenty pages every month, and because there is a very substantial Mexican-American community on the West Side, a number of articles appear in Spanish as well as English.

The West Side has a striking physiognomy, divided into a flood plain and a steep escarpment. Approached from the downtown section of St. Paul by the Wabasha Street Bridge, the steep craggy cliffs—their base defaced by a clutch of billboards—seem to cry out for an environmental impact statement. For generations from the middle of the nineteenth century the river flats were the first home of the poorest of newly arrived immigrants. First came the waves from Ireland and the German-speaking countries, and from 1880 to 1920 Jews arrived from Eastern Europe. Syrians and Lebanese added to the mix of cultures. Between 1940 and 1960 large numbers of Mexican-Americans who had been recruited to work in the Minnesota sugar-beet fields moved here.

A neighborhood much like the lower East Side in New York, the area was overcrowded, graced with the city dump nearby and no playground space for children. As late as the 1940s many homes were heated by kerosene. In St. Paul upward mobility is quite literal, for the flats, at the lowest point, were prey to continual flooding in

Robert Halladay

Temple of Aaron, 616 South Mississippi River Boulevard, St. Paul.

addition to other misfortunes. Residents moved upward to higher ground when their economic conditions improved.

But like the East Side of New York, the West Side flats sank their roots deep into residents' lives, for though this was the poorest of poor neighborhoods, a feeling of camaraderie existed and people who were born and raised here attested to a strong neighborhood feeling.

In 1956 the St. Paul Port Authority announced a plan to acquire the flats for the Riverview Industrial Park, on the grounds that the continual flooding made it an unfit area for homes. All residents were forced to sell their homes, some for as little as $2,000 or $3,000, and a community was uprooted. Unfortunately a bad taste has been left on the West Side, for public housing was not finished until some years after residents were forced to leave. And leaving meant not only losing shelter, and the only shelter very poor people had, but companionship and the host of emotional associations connected with a neighborhood. Ironically the flood wall now protecting the productive Riverview Industrial Park was never built for the people who merely had their homes on the West Side flats.

The most striking piece of architecture on the lower West Side today is the Torre de San Miguel housing project, with an Italianate campanile rising picturesquely from its midst. The tower is all that remains of St. Michael's Church, which burned some years ago. The federally funded housing project for low-income residents is one of the best designed housing projects in either city. It avoids the starkly cold look of concrete and brick, and through its use of wood siding placed at various angles and an interesting grouping of the townhouses with trees and patios, it has an inviting look.

The area shows a vast improvement since an increasing number of residents have been able to buy their own homes under various urban renewal programs. Formerly, absentee landlords allowed property to deteriorate, but now new pride is evident in spruced-up houses and lawns.

The streets leading up to the West Side Heights are alluringly steep, promising wonderful vistas and surprises. Regrettably, a large part of the upper West Side is drab. Many of the homes, particularly on the southern rim of the community, are small and crowded onto narrow lots. Belvidere Street has a clear view of an enormous scrap-iron area below. Small wooden and stucco homes are similar to the New Orleans shotgun homes, so called because they are one-room wide and if you shoot through the front door the pellets will emerge at the back door. Yet there is one quality that emerges. The slightly tattered look created by streets, many of them bereft of sidewalks, with small homes surrounded by picket fences and large trees, is much more like that of a small town than of a neighborhood in a city of over 300,000 people. The manicured lawns of the more affluent neighborhoods are not so prominent. The streets meander up and around the hills.

Throughout the heights large nineteenth-century homes remind us that this area once attracted wealthy residents. One of the most interesting houses is the Ossian-Strong house at 2 East George Street, a Wuthering Heights setting where the strength of the structure is achieved partly through the use of stone quoins at the corners and the long handsome windows. West Delos and Isabel streets are quiet, with spacious homes mixed in with more modest ones. The carriage house accompanying the house at 64 West Delos has enchanting gingerbread architectural detail.

Gemma Rossini Cullen

The West Side, St. Paul. Top, Victorian home on West Side Heights; center, Torre·de San Miguel Housing Project; bottom, castlelike building at the foot of the bluffs.

There are some quietly prosperous sections on Prospect Boulevard with Victorian homes which have a panoramic view of the downtown section of St. Paul. It is not a beautiful view, but distance, if not lending enchantment, lends—distance at least. There it is, car parks, commerce and industry, traffic arteries in every direction, and the beautiful Cathedral in the background.

Today the ethnic tapestry of the West Side of St. Paul can be detected in such commercial establishments as the El Burrito Bakery featuring baked goods with a Mexican bent, Morgan's Lebanese and Mexican Grocery Store, Manuel's Mexican Grocery, and the Astor Theater which features Spanish-language films two nights a week. A number of restaurants serve Mexican food and at 199 East Plato Boulevard is a Middle Eastern restaurant. The Coronado Tortilla Factory at Concord and State streets turns out eight hundred tortillas daily.

The Mi Cultura day care center is staffed with teachers who speak Spanish and English. The newly expanded bilingual program at a number of West Side schools was sorely needed in a community where many of the children come to school having heard little or no English at home and represents a victory for residents who were tired of seeing their children branded as slow learners when they were given lessons in a foreign language. Tied in with the program is a Mexican-American Resource Center in Roosevelt School.

Neighborhood House at Robie and State streets, which has been on the West Side for nearly eighty years, has a long history as a community center, in early years helping newly arrived immigrants learn English and with a later emphasis on recreation. Now part of the Concord Terrace Neighborhood Center, it continues to attract diverse ethnic strands. It embraces a nursery school, community education, a health clinic, as well as being deeply involved in desegregation efforts for the local public schools.

The Migrant Tutorial Program is one more manifestation of the determination of residents to raise standards of education. It serves not only children of migrant workers but others who in the first few years of school need help in math, reading, and spelling. Federal funds provide staff salaries, but the program is heavily dependent upon volunteers who work on a one-to-one basis with the children. Half of the volunteers are bilingual since many of the children come from Spanish-speaking families.

Like the West Side, the East Side of St. Paul is hilly and has a long history. The Dayton's Bluff neighborhood on the East Side, one of the oldest in St. Paul, was named for Lyman Dayton, a realtor who built his home here in St. Paul's salad days as a river town. Chief Justice Warren Burger came from this neighborhood and Justice Harry Blackmun lived here as a child. As boys they would have had panoramic vistas, for the Dayton's Bluff area has some of the most spectacular views of the river and the flood plain in either city, although it is somewhat marred by commerce and industry. Once an elegant residential section, the Bluff neighborhood today retains vestiges of its former grandeur in a number of large homes such as that at 196 Mounds Boulevard and the princely turreted red brick residence at 827 Mound Street. The neighborhood is a curious mixture of modest bungalows, some more substantial but not large homes, and an occasional truly desolate structure with all the signs of decay. And this is strange since in addition to the river views, Dayton's Bluff contains the Indian Mounds Park with its generous expanses of open space. But part of the answer may lie in the building of a freeway nearby which now detracts from the neighborhood's attractions.

North of the Dayton's Bluff area, the St. Paul Overall Laundry is well placed at Kenny Road and Payne Avenue as the Payne-Minnehaha neighborhood has long been a blue-collar residential area. It contains some of the oldest homes in either Minneapolis or St. Paul. At 485 Kenny Road is the home built in 1855 by Benjamin Brunson, surveyor of the city of St. Paul. But the most famous landmark within the Payne-Minnehaha section is one no longer inhabited, Swede Hollow, a steep ravine paralleling Payne Avenue. In 1841, Edward Phalen, an adventurous young immigrant from Ireland, was freed from jail after having been accused but not convicted of murdering a compatriot. Phalen staked a claim in the hollow area and the creek which flows through it now bears his name (as does nearby Lake Phalen). The hunters and trappers who followed him found it a convenient place for their trade as well as fine shelter. When the Swedish immigrants poured into the city in the 1850s some of them moved into shacks abandoned by the hunters. Later came the Irish, the Italians, and the Mexicans. Tales of the hollow resemble those of the West Side flats, for it remained a poor man's first stop, but one which evokes loving as well as harsh memories. Men from Swede Hollow worked on the railroads and in Hamm's Brewery, which is still one of the major employers on the East Side. But nothing was done to provide the hollow with proper sewers and in 1956 its contaminated water supply was declared a health hazard. The shacks were burned after the handful of remaining residents were evicted. Today, Phalen Creek runs largely underground and Swede Hollow is being cleaned up and turned into a city park.

On lower Payne Avenue near Swede Hollow, Yarusso Brothers Liquors and Italian Foods, Morelli's Supermarket, and Geno's Restaurant point to the neighborhood's years as an Italian colony. Like the Neighborhood House on the West Side, the Merrick Community Center has had a long history as a social service agency, in its early days helping new arrivals. The churches throughout the East Side had strong ethnic ties then, giving social and emotional support and serving religious needs.

On streets which climb and plunge St. Paul-fashion are narrow frame homes, sometimes brightened by much green paint, and with yards whose most notable characteristic is chain link fences. But in this land of tunnel winters when the absence of trees and other vegetation reveals the banality of much residential architecture, it is refreshing to find streets named Hyacinth, Magnolia, Geranium, and Rose. A few old mansions remain such as that at 543 Jessamine, but even up on the heights almost all the homes are small and unprepossessing. The sleek high-rise apartment house for senior citizens at 1000 Edgerton appears peculiarly out-of-step with the backyards of the homes around it, and nearby a huge automobile dump wounds the eastern rim of the area.

The Payne Avenue business district resembles a New England milltown with its low profile, small stores, and down-at-heels demeanor. If you glance to right or left onto adjoining streets sheds will be seen in some backyards. The business district was once a thriving commercial center, but today strip joints, bars, and antique shops have replaced many

Heidi Schwabacher

Farmers' Market, 312 Lakeside Avenue, Minneapolis. One of the pleasantest places in which to shop for fresh fruits, vegetables, and eggs, not far from downtown.

of the stores which supply daily needs, although an old, diminutive department store hangs in there reminding us that Minneapolis and St. Paul are in some ways a mosaic of small towns.

In Southeast Minneapolis there is a grocery store so small that regular customers learn a particular choreography in order to accommodate themselves to the restricted space. Everyone seems to know everyone else, and when a newcomer arrives a visit to the store serves as a coming-out party. Characteristically, it is a family business run by two generations, where the neighborhood kids often land their first jobs. It is a totally undistinguished place visually. Its official name long ago faded from the sign, but no matter as everyone knows the real name is Don's, for the late proprietor who set the tone of welcome to the entire neighborhood. The display windows are jammed with free advertisements for lost cats, garage sales, meetings to improve the neighborhood, and forthcoming concerts by a Renaissance music group. On Saturdays customers can munch salami, cheese, and pickles as part of a free lunch. Residents who move away often return to shop here, for prices and ambience are equally appealing. In many ways the store sums up the Twin Cities. These are cities made up of neighborhoods, family-centered areas with an unvarnished down-to-earthness more typical than the glitter of the cultural centers.

Prospect Park Food Market, "Don's," Southeast Minneapolis.

In Medias Res

The City Beautiful movement of the late nineteenth and early twentieth centuries frequently manifested itself in a craze to raze the old, the out-of-step, and often interesting buildings, and to erect in their places monumental, classically oriented architecture in the hope that some of the glory of ancient Greece and Rome would rub off onto our lives. A new Athens, it was hoped, would magically appear. In the early years of this century one result of the City Beautiful movement was the decision to eliminate the old Minneapolis City Hall at the triangular junction of Nicollet and Hennepin avenues and to throw up a gateway to the city in the form of formally planted gardens, a fountain, and a colonnaded Roman pavilion cum comfort station. The project was completed in 1917 and the pavilion bore the inscription "More than her gates, the city opens her heart to you." Unfortunately, nearby the city's less affluent citizens were posing a question mark concerning what the heart of the city was all about. Block upon block of pawn shops, sleazy hotels, and unemployed people were an unpleasant reminder that a beautiful city must consist of more than a pretty park at its entrance.

In the 1950s in a move to achieve a More Beautiful City the Gateway Redevelopment Project was undertaken, the unseemly establishments were removed, and the portentous colonnade came down. But gone too is the lovely marble and bronze fountain, removed to Lyndale Park where it is an ornament to the Rose Gardens. The new Gateway Park is a cold pristine lacquered lady, one who discourages loitering, touching, or any familiarity for fear her makeup will be spoiled. Some beautifully arranged flowerbeds border a vast unshaded area of concrete, an anonymous high-rise condominium towers over all, and the roaring traffic on Hennepin Avenue completes the bloodless montage. The focal point of the Gateway is a geyser of colored water, a twenty-four-hour Old Faithful as formidable as the rest of the park. Like too many trendy developments in urban face-lifting, it is nice to visit—from a distance—but not to live with.

Northwestern National Life Insurance Company Building, 20 Washington Avenue South, Minneapolis, designed by Minoru Yamasaki.

However, there are compensations. From the Gateway Park the Northwestern National Life Insurance building designed by Minoru Yamasaki and completed in the early 1960s provides an inspiring entrance to the Nicollet Mall. Yamasaki planned his work as both entrance to the Mall and focal point from its south end. The portico is an entry to a latter-day Greek temple made of sixty-three white quartz aggregate columns which form a series of attenuated pointed arches. The slabs of Vermont verde marble inserted into the green-tinted windows are both visually satisfying and a sensible choice in a harsh northern climate. Yamasaki's design gave class to what was a very undistinguished downtown area. It is a refreshing relief to the glass envelopes which had begun to spring up through the cities in the 1950s and at night the floodlit columns make a statement of repose and harmony. The six-story building is far more human in scale than most modern office buildings. It serves as a graceful reproof to the premium placed on tall buildings erected only for economic reasons. In choosing to build it here, the Northwestern National Life Insurance Company reversed a trend of other large companies which have followed executives to the suburbs.

The Federal Reserve Bank is Northwestern's most distinguished neighbor, built with a flexible cable forming a catenary on the principle of the suspension bridge. Architect Gunnar Birkerts states that this principle makes the building very safe, because it can withstand structural deficiencies or local overloading. It is the world's first occupied structure to have a column-free span of 275 feet, so that each of the ten floors in the office towers has an unobstructed area of 60 by 275 feet, with secure areas underground. The visible part of the building is literally hung over the plaza.

One requirement placed upon the builders in the Gateway Area was that landscaped plazas must be provided. An eerily spacious slanting plaza on the north side of the Federal Reserve Building has inner-tube-like seats circling formally arranged trees. These forbidding, symmetrically arranged benches were meant to attract downtown strollers and to be used for outdoor concerts. But it is noteworthy that few people sit there—and anyone who has tried them will soon know why. The unemployed with much time and little money choose to sit on the library benches on Nicollet Mall. To see the sculptural embellishments in the Federal Reserve Plaza, Paul Granlund's *Time Being* and Charles Perry's *Thrice*, the walker must ascend the concrete void. The Federal Reserve Plaza is a dismal failure; totally dehumanized, it is a windswept moonscape for robots, dangerous at night and uninviting in the daytime.

In the 1850s Joseph Nicollet, a brilliant and colorful astronomer-mathematician-cartographer, emigrated from his native France to Minnesota to explore Lake Itasca and to map much of the country between the Missouri and the Mississippi. Ironically, one of the many place names honoring this adventurer-scholar was Minneapolis's Nicollet Avenue, which by the 1950s had declined into a dingy, traffic-clogged downtown main street, apparently going the way of most central city shopping areas. Merchants were wringing their hands over the flight to suburban shopping centers and with good reason, for the suburban hucksters appeared temporarily more alluring.

To reverse this seemingly inevitable decline eight blocks of Nicollet Avenue were reworked into a pedestrian Mall. Financed by federal funds and

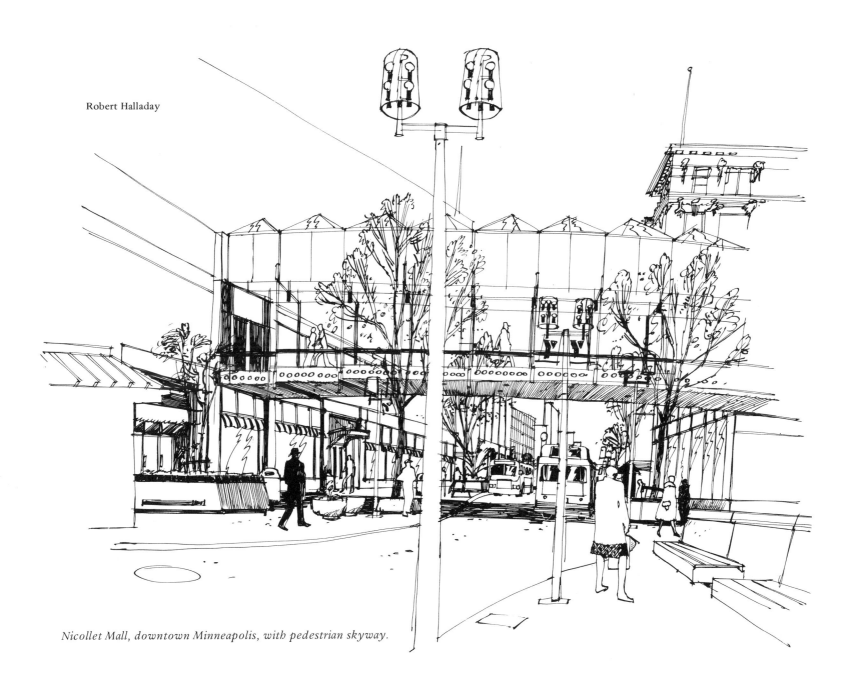

Robert Halladay

Nicollet Mall, downtown Minneapolis, with pedestrian skyway.

assessments on merchants in the area, the Nicollet Mall, completed in 1967, is the culmination of years of planning. While miracles could not be worked, designer Lawrence Halprin and Barton Aschman Associates converted a totally undistinguished street into a two-lane serpentine, a relief from the straight lines which prevail in much of the city. The two lanes retained for vehicular traffic were to be limited to an occasional emergency vehicle, but in reality police cars, taxis, city-owned vehicles, and an increasing number of buses defeat the original plan.

The idea of streets for people, a return to pedestrianism, had long been heralded by a number of writers such as Bernard Rudofsky and Jane Jacobs, who urged a commonsensical use of the street as a room. Aesthetically the Mall is a partial success. Its most appealing feature is the generous amount of space allotted to the wide, undulating sidewalks which have earth color terrazzo designs. All utilities are underground and street lights are at a level for pedestrians rather than cars. Trees, benches, and heated bus shelters were installed. On the other hand, some of the granite fountains are ungainly bathtubs, and there is about the total design a fussiness, a too eager attempt to make it a fun place. But in the summer, flowers and trees are refreshing.

As realistic urban planners the Mall designers are to be commended, for nothing was demolished to complete the design. Main street was reworked, not destroyed. This is not without problems since the existing façades were anything but stylish. Dayton's steadfastly retains two mismatched, dirt brown façades on the Mall. Though complying with the Gateway insistence on plaza space in new construction, the Northern States Power Company threw up an urban fortress. And most of the existing buildings simply fade from memory through sheer lack of style.

Though most of the Mall buildings antedate the revamping of the street, one midget monstrosity in the form of Mount Vernon colonial has been wedged into a section of the block between Eighth and Ninth streets. Here was an opportunity to erect an interesting building, and to commission a fine piece of sculpture, but the Bank of Minneapolis chose instead to foist upon us this remnant of ersatz nostalgia.

During the Middle Ages European man paid homage to God with earthly temples symbolizing the heavenly city of Jerusalem. Gothic cathedrals attained ever greater heights and their frames became thin skeletons of stone filled with vibrant and many-hued stained glass. In them the human being is dwarfed by the total effect. In our own century we have proclaimed our aspirations with glass towers piercing the sky to dwarf midget man and it is not entirely fanciful to note the similarity between such buildings as the IDS Tower and the great Gothic cathedrals. In Chartres the cathedral dominates the skyline of the town and, just as it can be seen from the fields of the Beauce, our blue-sheathed, fifty-seven-story cathedral imposes itself from any approach to central Minneapolis, seeming to arise out of a prairie. The comparison is particularly apt here because there are so few buildings of great height. The European cathedral was the dominant member of a group of buildings including the bishop's palace, a hospital, a school, and a cloister, and on major feast days the populace gathered there. Similarly, the IDS complex occupies a city block housing a hotel, several restaurants, an office building, a Woolworth's store, and, at the center of

Gemma Rossini Cullen

Crystal Court, IDS Center, Minneapolis.

it all, a Crystal Court, the nave of our latter-day cathedral.

Resemblances to more nearly contemporary structures also emerge, chiefly to the gallerias of Milan and Naples. The chief attraction of the court is that it is a place in which to walk around, to look into shop windows, perhaps to sit and read a newspaper, but above all, to watch the other watchers and walkers. It is also a point of confluence for the covered aerial walkways at the second-story level. Frequently groups of children are shepherded through on urban field trips. Today they might sit on the floor—and there always seems to be enough space—in order to write their observations. Some days a jazz band plays or a chamber chorale sings. A Ping-Pong table appears and players ignore kibitzers. Whatever the mix, there is one and it works. If not something for everyone, at least there is an ever-changing show.

The constant movement of humanity is enhanced by the design of the court, which is pentangular with "zogs" that echo the cutback sides of the Tower. Balconies are obliquely angled, and the four entrances to the court are placed asymmetrically in relation to one another. The naturally lit court is covered by honeycombed glass blocks which provide an interesting texture. Even on a dark winter's day there is ample light. Designer Philip Johnson has said that it is more like a glass birdcage than a glass envelope. As the onlooker stares upward on one side the Tower (of Babel?) appears to stretch to infinity, while on the other side the nineteen-story hotel has a comfortable finite look. For sitting, there are white cubes placed around pots of flowers and greenery, and though I could wish for some backing to the seating arrangements, they are an acceptable solution to the need for a gathering space and a place to watch the whorl go by.

One block away from the much lauded Mall is a very different world, teeming with a funky life. 'Tis probably imagination, but I swear an entirely different set of people walk on Hennepin Avenue. It is almost as if there were a higher priced admission onto Nicollet Mall. Visually, Hennepin is our Times Square, with a liberal endowment of porno bookshops, a string of first-run movie houses, saunas and steam baths, sleazy-looking hotels and some nineteenth-century buildings remaining from its better days. In recent years Hennepin is more or less ignored in favor of its dolled-up neighbor or hits the news largely for the periodic cleaning up of people who offer their wares not very subtly. But here is a feisty conjunction of history and honky-tonk, once the hub of the business district which sported the West Hotel, the largest in the city.

Wrapped around the corner of Fifth and Hennepin, the nine-story Lumber Exchange was the tallest office building in the city in 1885 when it was built to accommodate the boom-time need for office space. Now a wig of several more stories has been added, but the somber old girl hangs in there still with a massive Richardsonian entryway and Victorian bay windows doing a stately contrapuntal dance to the ground-floor adult book shop, steam bath, and Piggy's restaurant. Down the street at the corner of Hennepin and Sixth is the all-time, all-around eclectic prize, the Merchandise Building, formerly the Masonic Temple and dating from the 1880s. Another (and more elaborately carved) Richardsonian arched entryway, tourelles, Egyptian palm capitals, and classicized columns make a wonderful stew. At the bus stop in front is an equally eclectic crowd: Here is Mrs. Sairey Gamp, there two refugees from a Guindon cartoon; a doubtful pair of gauchos in oversized sunglasses had best be sidestepped; business people and dungareed youths pass by; a frowzy blonde on the wrong side of seventy and a galoshed man with an enormous shopping bag of food just purchased at the Great Northern Grocery, itself unlike other city groceries. This rundown aging emporium is like the rest of Hennepin, attracting a motley crowd to its jam-packed store.

The Minneapolis City Hall designed by Long and Kees and built between 1889 and 1905 reveals the pervasiveness of H. H. Richardson's influence on nineteenth- and early-twentieth-century architecture. Its strong central clock tower is a major landmark on the city skyline, although the monumentality of the building as a whole is somewhat diminished by the many new, more grandiose local buildings, particularly its sibling, the Hennepin County Government Center completed in 1974. Fortunately in designing the new Government Center the architects, John Warnecke Associates, chose to tie in the old with the new by the use of the same granite from Ortonville, Minnesota. The newer building serves to draw attention to the quiet grandeur and strength of the older one. The municipal building with its steeply pitched roofs and gables is a relief from the determinedly "fun" approach of much twentieth-century work. The "stoniness" of the granite is purposely emphasized and reflects the Teddy Rooseveltian manliness of the period.

The new Hennepin County Government Center has the solidity without the stolidity of the older building. It is actually two separate buildings, one serving the county administration and the other as courthouse for municipal, district, and probate

Robert Halladay

Minneapolis City Hall, left, and Hennepin County Government Center.

85

cases. The towers are tied together by an atrium, at twenty-four stories the tallest in the Western Hemisphere. To cover the space between the buildings is a sensible idea, but there is something awkward about such a high atrium. The glass walls which tie the towers together are crisscrossed by structural beams covered with porcelain, a startling change from the glass envelope architects have used in recent years. Beams are seen throughout the atrium. Outside of the buildings there is a formal, rather cold plaza on the north while the south side has a fine plaza dressed with linden, birch, and flowering crab apple trees.

Within the Government Center demountable partitions divide a floor so that it can be rearranged for changing needs. The new county boardroom, designed to be soundproofed from the waiting area, is visible to outer areas and the meeting in progress is piped out to the waiting room. Possessing as lush a late-in-the-century interior as could be found in any commercial boardroom, it features purples, magentas, and rust brown. Immediately behind the commissioners' handsome chairs a yellowish onyx screen brings to mind a little theater, a Hollywood set of the thirties. One expects that any moment Jean Harlow will pop out in one of her negligees!

Minneapolis and St. Paul have made their share of appalling errors in leveling apparently outmoded buildings in favor of what is architecturally à la mode. Unquestionably the furor over the razing of the Metropolitan Life Building in downtown Minneapolis in the early 1960s received the most notoriety, and justly so for this structure, with a fine interior court, could well have served the city for generations. One outstanding renovation of this endangered species in downtown Minneapolis is the building now known as Butler Square, originally a warehouse designed by Harry Jones and completed in 1906. Jones fashioned wine-red brick into a massive Tuscan fortress palace, using amazing restraint for the period, and his beautiful façade has been left almost intact. The interior has been transformed into a handsome array of tiered shops and offices around an atrium, and an irregularly shaped skylight has been cut into the ceiling. Materials were restored and wherever it was necessary to remove them, they were reused in other parts of the building. The atrium was created by cutting away the floor membrane and leaving post and beam framing exposed, and the interior was sandblasted to bring out the rich, rough-hewn condition of the beams. The original materials have been beautifully blended with the warm colors and an abundant use of greenery. A Tuscan fortress palazzo may seem out of place in the flatland of the Mississippi Valley, but Butler Square is one of the few really impressive buildings in downtown Minneapolis.

What amazing confidence the business community must have had to hire a LeRoy Buffington to design a Florentine palazzo flour mill, a Yamasaki to do a Greek temple for the dull old insurance business, a Philip Johnson and John Burgee to build a glass birdcage for the investment business, and a Harry Jones to erect a Tuscan fortress to house the wares of this blatantly commercial city!

Inside Orchestra Hall at Eleventh Street and Nicollet Avenue are two stone reliefs of lyres nailed over the box office. They are the only vestiges of the Lyceum Theater (a building in which the symphony played in its early years) which was razed to make way for the first permanent home for the Minnesota Orchestra. The lyres are a reminder of many buildings like the Lyceum, built as

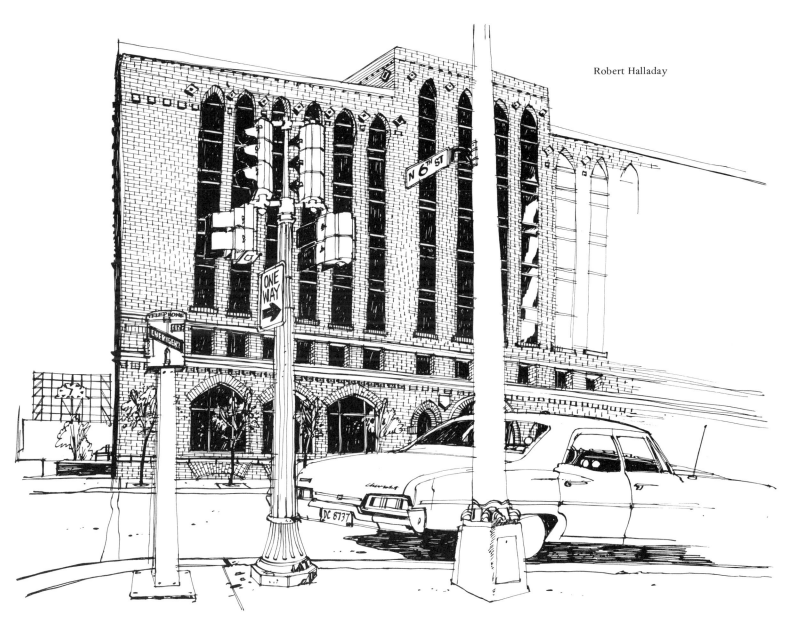

Robert Halladay

Butler Square Building, 100 North Sixth Street, Minneapolis.

all-purpose auditoriums where so many compromises were made in the attempt to accommodate lecturers, orchestral music, opera, and theatrical productions that no one purpose was very well served. Orchestra Hall is aptly named, for it was built for one reason, as a superb place in which to listen to music.

The lobby—with oversized exposed yellow air conditioning and heating ducts, magenta floor carpeting, and green ceiling beams—suggests a space ship, an ocean liner, or a boiler room. From the third tier particularly, there is the feeling of being on a transatlantic ship with narrow walkways, a maze of stairs, and exposed pipes. A product of the "let it all hang out" school of design, the lobby bears a remarkable similarity to the lobby of the Berlin Philharmonic Hall built between 1956 and 1963. In the university's Northrop Auditorium, for many years the home of the orchestra, the great vault of the stately old lobby imparted a subdued air to the vast crowds it accommodated. In contrast, the gangway levels of the Orchestra Hall lobby exude a vitality and excitement associated with a significant musical event.

The sound lock structure of the building consists of three parts, an outer lobby, a ring corridor, and the auditorium. The auditorium is separated from the ring by a one-inch air wall. Passing from the brash lobby through the muted ring to the auditorium is like passing into a surrealistic world, for the soothing salmon-colored seats and tiers contrast with the offwhite, uneven cubes which seem to make the ceiling and stage backing literally move. The cubes contribute to the acoustical perfection of the hall, for they disperse the sound effectively as a modern equivalent of uneven surfaces in the lavishly sculpted baroque concert halls of Europe. Not so obvious is the white oak paneling of the walls and wooden floors, which is the finest material acoustically. Balconies are extremely narrow, perhaps rather frighteningly so for the vertiginous concertgoer, but the acoustical gain of the narrowness is considerable. The size of the hall is ideal for concerts—twice as long as wide, seating 2,573 people.

Peavey Plaza, the out-of-door embellishment for Orchestra Hall, has been adorned with fountains of varying shapes and sizes. Perhaps the ungracious metal tubular fountains were meant to blend with the funny fat blue steamship funnels on the exterior of the Hall. But the plaza is largely satisfying with its pleasingly intricate number of levels, greenery, and a reflecting pool. It forms a connecting link in the extension of Nicollet Mall toward Loring Park.

Together the Walker Art Center and The Guthrie Theater, near Loring Park at the edge of downtown Minneapolis, make up the most widely known cultural complex in the cities. The exterior of the Guthrie is a dowdy remnant of its earlier self, for originally it was appointed with a concrete frame which imparted a dynamic air, conveying the drama that the theatergoer would find inside the building. Unfortunately the façade was removed a decade after the theater was built. But Ralph Rapson's interior remains a wonderland of orange, white, and black lobbies with upside down lollipop lights hung at different levels. The multicolored, asymmetrically arranged seats in the theater itself echo the drama on the thrust stage.

In the last decade of the nineteenth century, lumber baron Thomas Barlow Walker opened the Walker Galleries in downtown Minneapolis, a curiosity crammed full of oriental porcelains, pot-

Gemma Rossini Cullen

Orchestra Hall, 1111 Nicollet Mall, Minneapolis. Center right, auditorium; lower right, Peavey Plaza.

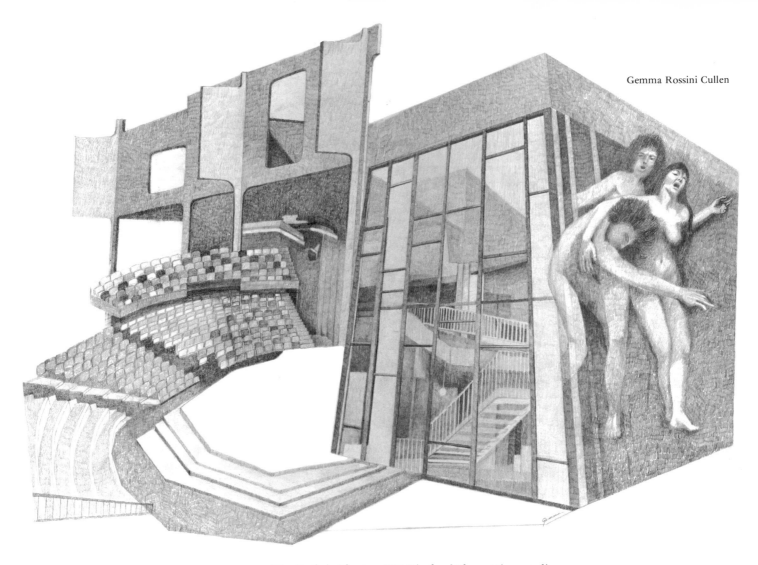

Gemma Rossini Cullen

The Guthrie Theater, 725 Vineland Place, Minneapolis.

tery, Persian carpets, jades, ceramics, and senti-mental paintings. Several homes and some decades later, the Walker Art Center is now housed in a superb building designed by Edward Larrabee Barnes and completed in 1971. Over the years, what had started as a private collection reflecting the whims of a wealthy dilettante has developed into one of the finest modern art collections in the country. The Walker now owns sculptures by Claes Oldenburg, David Smith, and Louise Nevelson and paintings by major American artists such as Robert Rauschenberg and Andy Warhol.

The exterior of the present building is a lavender monolith in elegant warehouse style, a stern de-scendant of the Moorish façade which graced the previous building in its early years. And the inter-

Gemma Rossini Cullen

Walker Art Center, with St. Mark's Cathedral as seen from sculpture terrace of the Center. At left, Alexander Calder's Octopus.

91

ior is the direct antithesis to the original Walker Galleries; here space is the operative word. Barnes created living and breathing room for large-scale works, and nowhere is there a sense that something was jammed in. The narrow, high lobby is ideal for such dramatic works as *Carousel Merge* by Sam Gilliam, a brilliant piece suggesting a curtain rising upon the drama of the art museum. Barnes designed seven rectangular galleries which radiate from a central core containing a passenger elevator and stairway. This series of ascending galleries leads the visitor from one startling exhibit to another, and galleries temporarily closed for new installations can easily be bypassed. Three outdoor sculpture terraces, with such works as Alexander Calder's *Octopus* and Jacques Lipschitz's *Prometheus Strangling the Vulture*, can be seen against the backdrop of the city. Nearby are the neo-Gothic St. Mark's Episcopal Cathedral, the Hennepin Avenue United Methodist Church, and St. Mary's Roman Catholic Basilica—the latter now stranded like a great whale on a beach of highways.

But what characterizes most of downtown Minneapolis is the absence of character. Buildings fail to arrest one's attention. Near the Hennepin County Government Center the Grain Exchange with its terra-cotta medallions of ears of corn—our indigenous art—is an echo of Louis Sullivan's Wainwright Building in St. Louis, and the Flour Exchange and Pittsburgh Plate Glass Building are also worth attention, but they are all in such a no-man's-land that there is nothing to bring the average visitor here. One block from Nicollet Mall is Marquette Avenue, the commercial banking street, a succession of dreary façades with nothing to either attract or repel. The poor old Foshay Tower —once touted as a star, the highest building in town—never did have much to say for itself. The Northwestern Bell Telephone's art decorama is best mercifully ignored. The bombed-out look created by parking lots is a depressing spectacle around the fringe. Beyond the Mall's northern end and screening the river is the WPA-style post office. The Great Northern Railroad Station in stately classical garb is nearly drowned out by Minneapolis's real contribution to pop art, an enormous Grain Belt beer cap blinking like a middle western equivalent of Doctor T. J. Eckleburg's eyes in *The Great Gatsby*. What use all the IDS towers, Yamasaki buildings, and renovations of Nicollet Island when electric bottle caps and billboards are permitted to tie upon us a Hick America tag?

Two grandly sited buildings, the State Capitol and the Cathedral, vie with one another for preeminence overlooking the downtown section of St. Paul from the north. The somewhat higher elevation of the Cathedral of St. Paul once called forth comments about the primacy of temporal or spiritual governments here, but speculations aside, there is no question about which is the more impressive building architecturally. Emmanuel Masqueray's Cathedral has a tension, vitality, and compactness sadly lacking in Cass Gilbert's sprawling, déjà vu Capitol. This magnificent baroque structure, completed in 1915, is a culmination of high hopes for the Roman Catholic population of this area, anticipated some seventy-five years earlier when Father Lucian Galtier had built a log church "so poor it would well remind one of the stable at Bethlehem" and, in his own words, "blessed the new Basilica which was dedicated to St. Paul, for he was the apostle of na-

Terra cotta relief on Grain Exchange Building, Fourth Avenue at Fourth Street, Minneapolis.

tions.'' Like so many of the city's early structures, the first church was on lower land, near the river. A marker locating Father Galtier's aspiring basilica can be seen today at the busy intersection of Kellogg Boulevard and Minnesota Street.

Masqueray, like his mentor Richard Morris Hunt, was imbued with the beaux-arts devotion to archaeological correctness and the glory of past styles. Baroque architecture, very much a product of the Counter-Reformation of the sixteenth century, was a tangible symbol of God's glory and the strength of the church. It is not surprising that Masqueray chose a triumphant architecture for the Archdiocese, with this magnificent site on which to build in a new land.

For many decades a peculiarly conformist notion that all public buildings must be versions of the architecture of ancient Rome was deeply imbedded in the American consciousness. Ancient Rome was at times a republic whose virtues could well be emulated in our brave new world, it was thought; therefore, imitating that republic architecturally should ensure a fulfillment of our ideals.

The scene has all the signs of a facetious culture,
Publishing houses, pawnshops and pay-toilets;
August and Graeco-Roman are the granite temples
Of the medicine men whose magic keeps this body
* Politic free from fevers,*
* Cancer and constipation.*

W. H. AUDEN

The "blandishment" architecture that swept through our cities and towns too often resulted in boringly repetitive public buildings. It is not surprising to find that six of the designs submitted for a new Minnesota State Capitol in the 1890s were, in one way or another, Roman structures with motifs from Caesar to Bernini. Cass Gilbert was awarded first prize for his T-square plan with a dome deriving from Michaelangelo's dome for St. Peter's. Ultimately, then, our "republican" State Capitol is really a building of the Roman Renaissance (not the most republican of times!). No doubt Gilbert and his fellow citizens saw anything from the eternal city as a badge of continuity and stability. What is clearly true is that the building was meant to announce that Minnesota had grown up; it was no longer a rural state on the edge of the frontier.

Directly below the attic at the base of the dome is a golden quadriga designed by Daniel Chester French and Edward C. Potter. It is no accident that by 1904 "Prosperity" was in the driver's seat, for the state had grown to a population of 1,751,394 in six decades, with 365,000 concentrated in the Twin Cities.

The ostentation of the exterior prepares us for the interior, but here the variety runs the gamut from some handsome areas and details, to amusingly naive choices, to blatant vulgaria. The Roman Imperial style demanded a rotunda, in this case one hovered over by lunettes featuring personifications of qualities thought to sum up the Northwest as a civilization. However, the sadly wooden, academic results are a symbol not so much of the Northwest as of a provincial fear of seeming provincial.

The monumental staircases, though wasteful, present some interesting vistas. At the second floor varicolored marble columns make a handsome gesture. The governor's office and reception room are a potpourri of pretension. Walls positively frosted with baroque carving and gold-leaf accents are glittered over by an Austrian chandelier. In contrast, the House of Representatives is charmingly elegant, a hemicycle with red walls, red carpeting, white pillars, and arabesques in the lunettes. Here the palatial grandeur is toned down. But on the whole our chief government building is a lavish spread—not doors, windows, stairs, or lights, but portals, fenestration, escaliers, and chandeliers!

Debates over the differences between the two cities no longer produce the outright venom of nineteenth-century one-upmanship (which at one point descended to falsifying population records), but today there is a feeling on the part of many St. Paulites that Minneapolitans have grown too big for their britches, and judging from the problem of financing some of the cultural institutions and downtown redevelopment, they may well be correct. What is clearly visible, even to the most casual, uninstructed visitor, is that the downtown area of each city is quite unlike that of the other. No one could mistake the canyoned and twistingly confusing assemblage of streets in downtown St. Paul for that of the eminently more practical and boring platting of the commercial core of Minneapolis. In St. Paul the pristinely laid out Capitol approach is belied by the jumble of buildings in the central business district. The towers of Assumption Church, the French Renaissance chateau Old Federal Courts Building, the stunning Osborn Building, and a goodly mix of other old churches and mercantile structures offer a pleasing variety. As you look from the Capitol toward the Veterans Service Building graced with Alonzo Hauser's fountain sculpture *The Promise of Youth*, a view of the river bluffs in the distance adds another dimension to

Robert Halladay

East Grand Staircase, Minnesota State Capitol, St. Paul.

95

House of Representatives, Minnesota State Capitol, St. Paul.

this downtown. From the Capitol the descent into the city is an exterior grand escalier. All the gateway parks in the world cannot do what nature did for St. Paul. One does not so much approach Minneapolis as sidle into it.

Below the Capitol and Cathedral rise the twin spires of a building antedating both, Assumption Church, completed in 1873. Although Minnesota is generally stereotyped as a last outpost of Sweden, more Germans than Swedes found new homes here in the nineteenth century, escaping the upheavals caused by the Revolutions of 1848 and the military conscriptions threatening in the 1870s. And as in the case of other Europeans, the lure of a better life materially drew them to the new Eden. A particularly large group settled in St. Paul, sometimes led on by the largely fabricated reports of Gottfried Duden and by agents for the St. Paul and Pacific Railroad. Other promoters like Senator George Becker had grandiose notions of a new Germany in Minnesota.

Although the handsome neo-Romanesque Assumption Church is no longer in a neighborhood parish it is an interesting reflection of the hopes and dreams of immigrants and a key to local history. These worshipers who had outgrown an earlier building hired the court architect to the ruling family of Bavaria to design their new church. Joseph Reidl's re-creation of the Ludwigskirche of Munich presents a stern counterpoint to the Cathedral flaunting its baroque glory on the hill above.

The big names in urban design touch down in Minneapolis with great frequency these days, where the Nicollet Mall, the IDS Tower, Orchestra Hall, and the Minneapolis Institute of Arts are potent drawing cards. But they would do well to visit Rice Park in downtown St. Paul for a look at

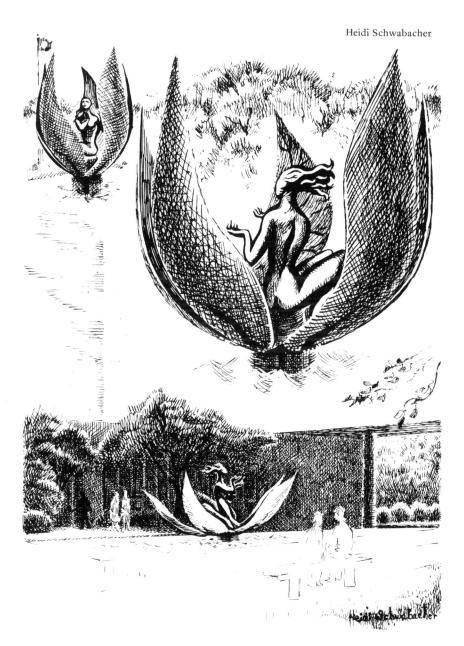

Heidi Schwabacher

The Promise of Youth *by Alonzo Hauser, outside Veterans Service Building, Capitol Approach, St. Paul. The fountain runs on a hydraulic system which causes the petals to open and close on a twenty-four-hour cycle.*

Gemma Rossini Cullen

Rice Park, with St. Paul Public Library in background. Center, The Source *by Alonzo Hauser.*

an outdoor room which did not come about as a result of a wholesale face-lifting. It is, moreover, an outdoor room which is used by St. Paulites without much fanfare from the local impresarios. In 1849 Henry Rice—who was to be one of our first United States senators, the man who presented the Minnesota state constituion to President Buchanan—donated 1.6 acres of land for a city square. Rice's park seems to have had its hillocks and declivities in fashion and appearance, for in the 1860s and 1870s neighborhood women found it a convenient spot in which to beat rugs, and cows frequently broke out of nearby yards and pastures to wander into its purlieus. Both were apparently driven out by 1883, when a reception was given here to mark the completion of the Northern Pacific Railroad and President Chester Arthur and Generals Grant and Sherman put in an appearance. After World War II Alonzo Hauser was engaged to design his figure *The Source* for a fountain which acts as a magnet during the warm weather. On the hottest days children simply wade in; others sit nearby to catch some coolness from the waters like the Romans who long ago discovered the psychological value of moving water in steamy weather.

The park has a number of fine shade trees and plenty of places in which to sit, none of them trendy tire seats. Nor is it a bloodless concrete wasteland. There are grass and flowers, and a softness about this open space. People eat their lunches, while others with time on their hands gravitate to the comfortable benches. Although not enclosed on all four sides, Rice Park gives the impression of being an enclosed space, an oasis much like European squares. Two of the "walls" are gracious revivals, the building housing the quietly dignified St. Paul Public Library and Hill Reference

Assumption Church, 51 West Ninth Street, St. Paul, with the Cathedral in the background.

Library, a marble Renaissance structure built around an open court, and the Old Federal Courts Building, in full Victorian French chateau bloom.

The old Fed nearly met up with a wrecking ball in the late 1960s before the city paid the Federal government $1 for it under the surplus buildings act of 1972. A new name, the Landmark Center of the Arts and Science Council, indicates the new tenants who undertook the herculean task of finding the means to renovate it. Now that the St. Cloud granite exterior has been cleaned up, the freewheeling Victorian interpretation of Loire Valley Renaissance architecture can be seen with its full complement of turrets, towers, and a variety of figures in relief—including a bat.

Cost had apparently been no barrier in outfitting these turn-of-the-century government buildings. Once more one can see the hand-carved Vermont marble fireplaces and the maple floors in the judges' chambers and the marble terrazzo floors elsewhere. Fine materials were not always a guarantee of taste; only the Victorians could have dreamed up that tiny fireplace with a too-large hood, reminding us of a Victorian parent threatening the fire-in-the-child with total extinction if any sparks escaped. Now under the umbrella of the Ramsey County-St. Paul Arts and Science Council, the courtrooms are frequently used for concerts given by the St. Paul Chamber Orchestra, an organization whose existence indicates how St. Paul has competed with Minneapolis. The most hospitable part of this grand old bosomy building is the inner court which has a new translucent roof with hanging gardens. Lunchers bring their food into the courtyard, a wintertime indoor park where they are entertained occasionally by music groups.

From Rice Park one can stroll to Kellogg Boulevard, a parkway paralleling the river from its bluffs. What an object lesson in the drift into debrisland the view provides! You would think that an uglification committee had sunk its tentacles deep into this city at an early stage. A montage of commerce and industry with a particular stress on oil storage tanks vies with an ugly drawbridge and the dramatic High Bridge for attention. Train tracks immediately below the boulevard parallel Shepard Road. The Northern States Power Building winks its ugly tower light and Harriet Island, once a fine recreation area, is now a dilapidated marina. The beautiful bluffs south of the river cannot be entirely obscured by the industrial and commercial mess.

Yet there is a fascination in the river which is very much here in downtown St. Paul, whereas its sibling, like a second generation hiding its lowly origins, turned its back on the Mississippi. True, Minneapolis has now rediscovered its colorful ancestor, but St. Paul has never forgotten it. And on a beautiful summer's day the *Jonathan Paddleford* and its companion the *Josiah Snelling*, sternwheelers built in the 1970s to feed the nostalgia craze, quietly churn their way upstream for a tour of the river to Fort Snelling. Downriver the Mississippi loops in a graceful arc encased on one side by green bluffs.

Along Kellogg Boulevard the simple stone monument to Father Lucian Galtier at Minnesota Street resides in a well-landscaped green; the city provides benches, shade trees, and grass for river watchers. The art deco County Courthouse, the Hilton Hotel, and other pleasant if not particularly distinguished buildings give a prosperous look to St. Paul's riverfront.

At the foot of Jackson Street Lambert's Landing was the lower landing, competing with the

Heidi Schwabacher

Old Federal Courts Building, 75 West Fifth Street, St. Paul, started in 1892 and completed in 1902.

101

Heidi Schwabacher

*New York Eagle Marker, southwest corner of
Jackson and Fourth streets, St. Paul.*

upper landing at Chestnut Street. During the heyday of riverboat traffic the lower landing became the terminus of the Red River Ox Cart Trail, on which ponderous vehicles carried buffalo robes, hides, and tongues, tallow, and pemmican, to be shipped downstream to the world after a journey of 448 miles from Pembina near the Canadian border.

Constant surprises await the explorer of hilly downtown St. Paul. These are not uniformly aesthetic successes, but the walker more frequently pauses for a new vista than in Minneapolis shod in its sensible flats. As Fifth Street ascends from Cedar the Garden Plaza adjoining the Osborn Building rivets attention with its collage of greenery and massive red metal sculpture against the backdrop of the fine soaring silvery Osborn Building. Liberman's sculpture is an unwelcoming futuristic piece, but the plaza space gains much from its site on a height above a hilly street. The Osborn Building, designed by Clark Wold and completed in 1968, is the most successful of St. Paul's newer structures. The less fortunate Northern Federal Savings and Loan Building adjoining it on Wabasha is dressed in that peculiarly eerie glass that suggests a fun house turned inside out.

St. Paul and Minneapolis are racing to build their networks of skyways, with St. Paul claiming that it will have the longest controlled-climate enclosed walkway in the United States when it is completed. Already it is possible to traverse a considerable distance, and in cold weather downtown workers can walk some blocks to lunch without an overcoat, reaching their destinations without arriving all polka-dotted from black slush. In St. Paul the Skyway Building with its shops along the way is a latter-day Ponte Vecchio. Rivalry aside, the skyways make sense in both cities: they do protect the walker from traffic and inclement weather, and are infinitely more civilized than tunnels. Some surprising sights turn up, particularly in hilly St. Paul—including the unbelievably boosterish tree atop the Midwest Federal Building, labeled "Growing with St. Paul," and two of the endangered species from the nineteenth century, the Endicott and Pioneer buildings on East Fourth Street.

The Endicott with its Italian palazzo façade in red pressed brick and sandstone, which was designed by the firm of Cass Gilbert and James Knox Taylor in 1889, is a handsome structure but is undoubtedly overlooked since it is on one of St. Paul's arroyo streets and somewhat dwarfed by the Pioneer Building next door. The walker in the city has to seek out the Endicott to appreciate its frieze and brackets, its lobby in pink marble, and stone-carved pilasters. The Pioneer Building is a successful remainder of the brown decades and one much to be admired for its strength and simplicity. Built in 1889, it has a beautiful wrought-iron spiral staircase and an open elevator shaft in its interior.

A few steps down the block at the corner of Jackson and East Fourth streets, a powerful bronze eagle protects her young from a snake and just as we nearly decimated our entire population of live eagles, we have done our best to level our architectural past. The eagle is proof of this, for it once enhanced another lavishly constructed office building, the New York Life Insurance Building at Minnesota and East Sixth streets. Although local historical societies made valiant efforts to keep the New York Building, it was razed in 1967. Designed and cast in the studio of the well-known sculptor Augustus Saint-Gaudens, the eagle is probably too often passed by in this corner of the downtown area. The Guardian Building at Minnesota and Fourth streets had walls five feet thick and every room was graced with outside light and air and its own fireplace. Now this building has gone too.

St. Paul's biggest building boom came in the decade 1888-1898 when eminent architects from New York, Boston, and Chicago were commissioned to design the most ambitious buildings. Now Metro Square, a cardboardy appearing beige and gray striped heap, and a Civic Center in the shape of a gas storage tank are pathetic descendants of those buildings.

Like Rice Park, Mears (formerly Smith) Park has been many things to St. Paulites. In 1849 it was donated to the city by two land speculators from Illinois, Robert Smith and Cornelius Whitney, and by 1881 a stockade there was used to confine workhouse prisoners. Today—after suffering the inner city blues as the center of the warehouse district—it is a releasing agent, and with extensive refurbishing it has been transformed into an outdoor civic center. Terraced brick seating areas around a reflecting pool, a fine fountain, an outdoor stage, and a variety of grade changes allow a number of activities to take place at the same time. Lunchers from nearby offices eat and stroll here, and crafts fairs, art shows, and concerts have brought new life to the area. The fine old elms make a link with the past. Mears Park provides a focal point for the renovation of the Lowertown area in St. Paul and shows what imagination can do to make use of an old-fashioned city square.

The renovation of the old Noyes Brothers wholesale drug building into Park Square Court on the north side of the park is a partial success with specialty shops, crafts galleries, restaurants, and live theater. The refurbishing antedated that of the

more ambitious Butler Square in Minneapolis and was accomplished with far less money. A gallery for craftsmen, outfitted by the original proprietors at a minimal cost, is a fine example of the fruits of taste and hard work, but many of the shops are too highly seasoned with wrought-iron grillwork and other kitsch for a somewhat compact building. However, Park Square Court has proved a welcome gathering spot for shoppers and diners. In this insane climate it makes sense to have so many options under one roof.

Nearby at 366-368 Jackson Street the old Merchant's National Bank has been turned into a restaurant and office building. This amusingly pretentious candystick is more quaint than tasteful with its encrustations of a stonecutter's flowerful fancy, all jammed onto a narrow four-story building.

The rediscovery of the 1930s has tended to exaggerate the charms of much art deco architecture and in the case of the Minnesota Museum of Art the building itself is far less impressive than the tastefully appointed art shows. Nearby the lovely little Renaissance Ramsey County jail is one of St. Paul's quiet triumphs.

Nothing on the exterior of the art deco Ramsey County Courthouse and St. Paul City Hall is preparation for Carl Milles's *Indian God of Peace* in the lobby. Its likeness on highway billboards threatens to drive it into a déjà vu category before the newcomer has even arrived in the city, but no flatulent advertisement can do justice to the power of the thirty-six-foot Indian god carved of white Mexican onyx set in a somewhat Hollywoodish lobby of dark blue marble. Reminiscent of pre-Columbian sculpture, the indigenous subject

Robert N. Taylor

Indian God of Peace, by Swedish sculptor Carl Milles, in St. Paul City Hall-Ramsey County Courthouse.

evokes the timelessness of the first inhabitants of Minnesota.

Modesty can be engaging, but St. Paul tends to hide many of its plums such as Henry Moore's *Bone Woman*, which stands in the Seventh and Cedar streets entrance to Dayton's Department Store. The cramped entryway fails to do justice to Moore's spare attenuated abstraction of the human form. Shinkichi Tajiri's *Growth Tower* is literally hidden in the charming Wabasha Court, an elegantly designed "backyard" off Sixth and Wabasha. However, George Sugarman's sculptural complex of brightly colored aluminum confetti and streamers brightens up the First National Bank at Fifth and Minnesota streets.

Is downtown St. Paul more lovable than downtown Minneapolis, more of a big small town—or just dowdier? Aficionados of each city constantly use these terms. The YMCA at Ninth and Cedar streets in St. Paul has been known to have as a neighbor a billboard with a scantily clad lady promoting adult entertainment. Other surprising juxtapositions impress themselves upon the walker's view. Mickey's Diner resides at Ninth and Wabasha, and an astonishing number of bars announcing Phyllis ("just arrived from the Coast") crop up throughout the area, often as close neighbors to the most elegant shops. It comes as a jolt to look across Wabasha from the Osborn Plaza and find a supermarket. There is in St. Paul no central spine like the Nicollet Mall. The walker has nothing to direct his movement.

It is still possible to park on downtown streets close to shopping areas in St. Paul, but in Minneapolis you must walk many blocks or resort to a parking ramp. On many Saturdays St. Paul stores are so nearly empty that one wonders if St. Paulites hightail it up the river to Minneapolis which is always big-city jammed. And indeed, the vacant stores on some streets are ominous signs.

Yet several venerable commercial establishments seem impervious to this air of decay. Gokey's on Fifth Street, a mini-Abercrombie and Fitch, with its hunting supplies, boots, and expensive sports clothes, has about it the air of a private club. The customer who pays with cash is obviously not a member. Nearby at the corner of Fifth and St. Peter stands Frank Murphy's shop for women, a small but handsomely appointed purveyor of expensive clothes in quiet good taste that St. Paulites believe distinguishes their city from the nouveau riche next door. The shop is still owned and carefully run by Mrs. Frank Murphy, and a large number of customers from both cities are well known to the sales personnel. But the ambivalence of the city is seen here. Once a year a bonanza sale is held across the street in the kindly, old-fashioned Hotel St. Paul. On a freezing January morn before eight o'clock customers line up to await the opening of the doors. Local newspapers carry pictures of matrons madly undressing any old place in the ballroom to try on the $100 skirts and similarly expensive coats reduced seventy-five percent. At a recent sale, one clerk remarked, "Oh, my, they're just WALKING. I've never seen them WALK before. One year the first woman in started to run and before she got more than a few steps she tripped and fell. Would have been crushed, you know, except that she was smart enough to start rolling over as soon as she fell and was able to roll right under the table." Quiet good taste laced with middle western enterprise.

The Places in Between

One of the joys of exploring the Twin Cities lies in finding the unexpected charmer in unlikely places. Some of the visual gems hidden in the bins of imitations are not downtown and must be sought out. During a walk or drive through a dull neighborhood frequently a fine piece of architecture or sculpture will break through the creeping fog of mediocrity. In one of the most grindingly depressing sections of the Midway district of St. Paul Evelyn Raymond's family group, a relief sculpture at 1919 University Avenue, embellishes not only that building but the whole block. Similarly, her fine St. Austin on the church of St. Austin, 4050 Thomas Avenue North in Minneapolis, makes a counterstatement to an unimaginative neighborhood.

In an upper-middle-class neighborhood at 205 Otis Avenue in St. Paul the Prince of Peace Lutheran Church for the Deaf, designed by Ralph Rapson, is too easily passed by. The façade of this airy glass jewel box consists of a metal screen in which circles are intersected with crosses, while the most dramatic element is the cluster of three crosses of varying heights in front of the church.

Not all of the romantic fancy of nineteenth-century builders went into residential architecture. At 882 West Seventh Street, St. Paul, the Schmidt Brewery is an 1880s architectural brewer's yeast of crenelations and Moorishly striped rounded windows. The designer's fancy appears to have strayed from the Rhine to the Iberian peninsula, or farther south and east, but the building has a fine assertive jaunty air. The *St. Paul Pioneer Press* for December 25, 1887, remarked that the "five prominent institutions in every new born Western town are the school, the church, the general store, the newspaper and the saloon." If not exactly the vanguard of civilization, the brewing industry came early to St. Paul, pioneered by Theodore Hamm in 1856.

Cass Gilbert left his mark on the Twin Cities in many ways and some of his smaller commissions reveal a more thoughtful, less portentous side than the State Capitol and the university's Mall in Minneapolis. St. Clement's Church at Portland Avenue

Gemma Rossini Cullen

Jacob Schmidt Brewing Company, 882 West Seventh Street, St. Paul.

Gemma Rossini Cullen

Right, Evelyn Raymond's Family Group *on Mutual Service Insurance Companies Building, 1919 University Avenue, St. Paul, formed from one and a half tons of hand-hammered copper. Ms. Raymond is the only living Minnesotan with a work of art in the Capitol Hall of Statuary in Washington, D.C. Left, Minnesota families, past and present.*

tecture seems quite right for its setting at the foot of Ramsey Hill, as if the church were in a Swiss village. It is a small limestone building with an asymmetrical assemblage of picturesque elements, including an extremely narrow spire at one side and a curving flight of steps suggestive of a steep mountainside. Some years ago the congregation disbanded and the building has at various times been home to a funeral parlor, an architectural firm, theatrical groups, and a dance studio.

You show us Rome was glorious, not profuse
And pompous buildings once were things of use.

ALEXANDER POPE

When the Minneapolis Institute of Arts was built between 1913 and 1915 it faced Fair Oaks, one of the city's few grandiose mansions, home of William Drew Washburn, nineteenth-century milling tycoon. Stylistically, Fair Oaks was a bit of everything, with stepped gables vying with a Gothic tower, bay windows, and a crypt-style porte cochere for attention. It was the McDonald's of great house architecture, for Washburn evidently thought to have the works, the Big Mac hamburger architecturally speaking.

During the early years of this century Imperial Roman structures were seen as the proper domiciles for Culture as well as for government and the New York firm of McKim, Mead and White which was engaged to design the institute building was turning them out in great numbers. A forbidding flight of steps led up to the original façade, the expectable classical portico announced that the visitor was now entering the Church of Art, and the rotunda within either frightened him off entirely or reassured him that all was well, that the vul-

and Milton Street in St. Paul is a re-creation of the village parish church found throughout England, with a hammer beam ceiling and a lychgate, a covered wooden gateway traditionally a resting-place for a coffin at the entrance to the churchyard. A variation on the picturesque English village church is a building that once housed the German Presbyterian Church. Designed for a group of German-speaking immigrants in the late nineteenth century, Gilbert's choice of Swiss mountain archi-

Gemma Rossini Cullen

Minneapolis Institute of Arts,
2400 Third Avenue South, Minneapolis.

gar outside world was walled out. In the interior, more monumental staircases and galleries with exceedingly high ceilings and poor lighting have been the despair of curators.

Grandiose in scale, this small central fragment was only part of the original much more ambitious plan, although an addition was made in the 1920s. It was not until the early 1970s that the long-awaited expansion was begun, when the Minneapolis Society of Fine Arts launched a drive to raise $32 million, engaging Kenzo Tange of Tokyo to add new wings on the south, east, and west. A symbol of the change in attitude toward art and art institutions is Tange's use of "borrowed scenery," for as one looks north from inside the cluster of downtown buildings form a backdrop symbolic of the changed attitude. Fair Oaks Mansion with its declaration of conspicuous consumption for the privileged few had long since been razed and its lovely rolling grounds designed by Frederick Law Olmsted are now a public park, where children sled in winter and run in summer and which all neighborhood residents use. The new wings open up to the whole city, bringing it into the Church of Art.

The old entrance, with a *noli me tangere* attitude engendered by the grand escalier, has been succeeded by a more easily accessible entrance on Third Avenue, and while the old façade remains unchanged, the doors are locked. True, Ernst Barlach's sculpture *Fighter of the Spirit*, now splendidly sited outside the new entrance, indicates a kind of guardianship, but it surely is not meant to ward off the uninitiated visitor.

Tange's well-defined white-glazed bricks give subtle texture to the exterior and interior walls. The much increased gallery areas were designed by Elena and Massimo Vignelli to focus on the art, not the interior architecture, and the modern heat and humidity controls ensure preservation of works of art as does the tinted glass of windows and doors. The glass see-through cases give the illusion that many works are freestanding.

A sculpture collection in the introductory gallery features braille labels for the visually impaired. In fact, any visitor is allowed to touch the superb works in this gallery dating from the sixteenth to the twentieth century. Throughout the museum, vistas are opened up. For example, from the decorative arts collection the visitor can see a seventeenth-century altarpiece. Many of the best characteristics of the old building have been preserved, such as the beautiful parquet wood floors in the galleries and the pink Tennessee marble in the halls. The lovely fountain court near the rotunda is the most gracious reminder of the opulence of this first building. Unfortunately the outside sculpture court between the new wings freezes the blood. Olmsted's graceful Fair Oaks Park, where the art conceals art, points a contrast and poses a question about our own developments in landscape architecture.

If anything in the Fine Arts Park heralds a new age it is the Children's Theatre. The story of its beginnings in the backroom of an Italian restaurant in the early 1960s and its peregrinations to other makeshift quarters is well known to city residents. When I took my sons to performances in 1962 the theater was temporarily performing in an abandoned police station and we took turns breathing with the other members of the audience. It is reassuring to see the American penchant for success applied to such a worthwhile group, and the $4.5 million theater plant must be the most glorious place in the world to be introduced to drama.

Gemma Rossini Cullen

Children's Theater, 2400 Third Avenue South, Minneapolis.

Designed so that no member of the audience is very far from the stage, it is a deep well of steeply banked seats, much like a Roman amphitheater such as that at Fiesole, above Florence. Even from the last row the most minute member of the audience can see and hear the performers on the traditional, proscenium-arched stage.

The designers left lots of space for squirming and especially for kicking. Before performances members of the company are apt to hawk oranges and lemons in nineteenth-century London cockney style, so that there is no pressure to act sedate. It is not a hushed temple for drama. The lobby area, carpeted in a lush claret color, is spacious, and during the winter the borrowed scenery of snow adds to the festive air.

The Fine Arts Park—which also includes a new home for the Minneapolis College of Art and Design—has called so much attention to itself that it is now attracting a number of jibes as a "shopping center" for the arts, with everything in one block. One reassuring thing is that there was no attempt to rebuild the whole complex in a more affluent section of the city. It is in the Whittier neighborhood, a curious area where many buildings are rundown while remaining nineteenth- and twentieth-century mansions attest to its earlier grandeur. The George Chase Christian residence now housing the Hennepin County Historical Society, the Italianate Edward Gale home, and the two mansions formerly owned by the Pillsbury family add charm to the area.

The Charles Pillsbury residence at 100 East Twenty-second Street might serve as a quiet counterpoint to the Burbank-Livingston-Griggs mansion in St. Paul. Here too revivalism held the day in design and the interior was outfitted with materials from European castles, but the Pillsbury mansion fared better under the surer taste of architects Hewitt and Brown and the interior design of Charles Duveen of London. Its exterior of dressed limestone has high gables characteristic of Jacobean buildings, stone mullions, and leaded-glass windows with seventeenth-century medallions from churches and castles. All of these features point to a longing for the grace and apparent stability of an earlier day. The home is quite lovely in its restraint. Duveen's choice of pegged teakwood flooring and oak paneling from English manor houses has a lasting richness. The low relief in the molded plaster ceiling is reminiscent of Robert Adam's eighteenth-century work.

Did bankers of yore feel that a vaultlike domicile was tangible proof of financial probity? The gloomy red sandstone fortress at 2116 Second Avenue South built in the late 1880s for Eugene A. Merrill, organizer of the Minnesota Loan and Trust Company, still keeps guard over Washburn-Fair Oaks Park.

The First Christian Church, erected in 1957, has a wooden ceiling reminiscent of Spanish churches and there are small colored roundels in its façade. It is a handsome addition to the Whittier area. Not far away at 2402 Fourth Avenue South is the 1874 home of the Frederick family, though now lapped by freeway grime, a rare specimen of a cupola house in Minneapolis. The Whittier neighborhood has some variety and is not a bad place to walk around in for a tour of the Minneapolis mix.

At the corner of Bloomington and Franklin avenues in Minneapolis is a grocery store which is apparently the ultimate step in urban warfare, for it has replaced its glass display windows with concrete blocks. But on the opposite side of Franklin

Heidi Schwabacher

Charles Pillsbury Mansion, 100 East Twenty-second Street, Minneapolis, built in 1914. A fine cartouche
and bas-relief embellish the semicircular eave space over the entablature to the porch.
Handsome lanterns grace the secondary entrance to the grounds.

Avenue stands a building that presents an alternative to the fortress grocery, the Native American Center, completed in 1975. It is the first urban community building erected for native Americans in the United States, and its warm cedar siding and low-lying, angling arms announce a different approach to urban problems. Built as a combined recreational, social service, and cultural agency, it is tangible proof that cooperation, dedication, and superior design have produced some of the most interesting architecture in the cities.

The Native American Center estimates that between 10,000 and 15,000 native Americans live in the Twin Cities area, with a very large concentration in this section of Minneapolis, the Phillips neighborhood. The problems of adjustment to urban life for those coming from the reservation have only recently been recognized by white citizens who set the pace and rules of the alien society into which native Americans must move. Too often new arrivals meet with Caucasian prejudice against dark-skinned people; prejudice of some landlords against the unemployed often means that substandard housing is the only dwelling place available; students are often confronted with teachers who do not understand Indian ways, and truancy is the predictable result. Other problems—locating a job and then finding recreational opportunities—present themselves.

During the sixties an increase in awareness of traditions in all groups led to an awakening to possibilities for improving lives. New opportunities from federal and local government grants to build community buildings led a number of native Americans in the metropolitan area to approach the City Council with a plan for a central building, which could house many needs. Members of the Urban American Indian Agency worked closely with the architectural firm of Hodne-Stageberg Partners in planning the building.

On the exterior artist George Morrison has adapted a crow quill pattern in designing the rough cedar siding. Natural wood and red, yellow, black, and white are used throughout the building, all with cultural significance. Cedar, fir, and burnished concrete blocks are highly effective aesthetically and the woods are as close as possible to their natural state. Twenty-five-foot pillars in the field house and museum reflect the twirling of the cardboard tubes into which they were poured.

The building as a whole is meant to reflect native American culture without attempting a direct re-creation of a specific type of structure. It is a reflection of the common tribal feeling, that of a community lodge. One area flows into the next; and with the exception of a few offices, the different levels are not shut off from one another.

Perhaps the spirit of the building is best expressed in the museum, for traditionally a museum is shunted off to a remote corner and swathed in protective silence to become a palace of culture, a palace which most people avoid. But the Native American Center's museum is a large open court so centrally located that the visitor is encouraged to pass through slowly, to look, to learn. Here is housed the permanent collection of cultural artifacts and a gallery for contemporary native American art. But it is a gallery with a difference. The angled ramps provide easy access for the handicapped and are a convenient area in which to hang works of art. Next to the museum and equally open is the library with publications, tapes, and albums relating to Indian life. The spirit of openness and welcoming is enhanced by the lack of

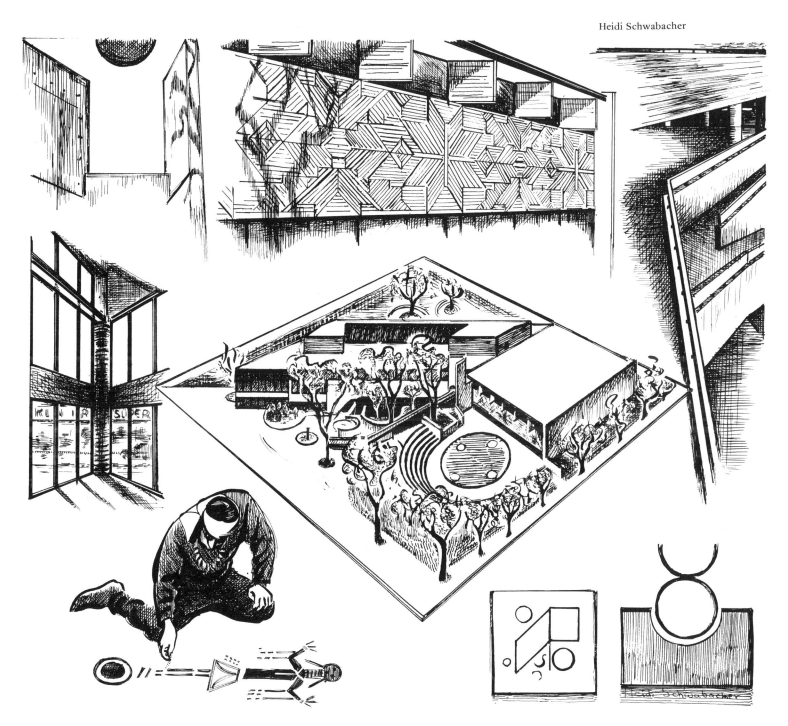

*Minneapolis Regional Native American Center, 1530 Franklin Avenue East. The circle motif throughout
the building and grounds has symbolic significance for native Americans. Top center,
collage in wood on the façade of building; lower left, a native American sand painting.*

rectangles here and in most of the building. In a world in which minorities have too often been forced into molds which have no relation to their cultures, the center offers a multitude of shapes, sizes, alternatives.

When I came to Minnesota some years ago, the first home I visited was one designed by Frank Lloyd Wright and built for Malcolm Willey on Bedford Street in Southeast Minneapolis. Wright, ever interested in employing unusual materials, here used Milwaukee sewer brick. The horizontality of the prairie is echoed in the long, low, one-story home with wide overhanging eaves, practical in this climate. A long wall at right angles to the house screens it from neighboring residences and in addition intensifies the feeling of horizontality.

Many of the features of the home are now so commonplace that they do not seem unusual, but when the house was built in 1934 it was highly revolutionary in several ways. A centrally located kitchen work area, adjacent to the living room, was a sensible recognition that the American middle-class family was becoming a servantless one, which no longer found it practical to hide the kitchen in the rear of the house. Wright defied the notion that Minnesota winters demanded a deep cellar foundation and successfully built the Willey home on a slab foundation.

Aesthetically the house, now owned by Harvey Glanzer, is still a highly satisfying one. The living room is designed with a tension and release technique: a seven-foot wall rises to a ten- and then to a twenty-foot brick wall. Cypress strips emphasize the contours of the ceiling rise. The varying planes of the brick wall and fine six-feet-high, six-feet-wide fireplace give texture to the winter focal point of the living room, while the glass wall of the opposite side makes the most of good weather. A brick patio at an odd but interesting angle appears to be a continuation of the brick floors in the living room, a result of Wright's interest in taking the indoors outside and bringing the outdoors into the home. All rooms have doors opening onto the patio, and the master bedroom has corner windows with a supporting post so that when the windows are open the ninety-degree aperture intensifies the indoor/outdoor feeling. The dictatorial Wright insisted upon designing furniture for his homes, believing that his ideas provided maximum flexibility for the use of the house in different seasons, and the house still contains a number of his chairs and tables.

Eliel Saarinen's last completed work stands at the corner of Thirty-second Street and Thirty-fourth Avenue South in Minneapolis—Christ Church Lutheran, completed in 1949. If I were to point to one building that stands out as the best of unostentatious architecture in the Twin Cities, this quietly dramatic building would be it. Saarinen and his son Eero worked within a tight budget to design this structure for a small corner-lot. Yet the soaring campanile with its brushed aluminum cross does not seem out of place in this somewhat mundane neighborhood. The texture of the brick exterior is exquisitely achieved with a variety of natural tones highlighted with dark red-wine bricks to give depth. On the stone façade sculptured figures representing the church, faith, hope, and love at work in the world are reminiscent of the rigid sculptures of early Gothic churches. But there is nothing forced about them and they are in keeping with the muted beauty of the building as a whole.

The focal point of the interior is the simple brushed aluminum cross on the altar which is lit by

Robert Halladay

Residence designed by Frank Lloyd Wright,
225 Bedford Street Southeast, Minneapolis.

natural light from one side. The subtle curve of the whitened chancel is both an acoustical and a visual achievement, putting the focal point of echoes outside of the congregation but also adding a pleasing asymmetry to the chancel wall. The northern clerestory wall undulates to absorb sound, but again provides a subtle variation in what is a largely neutral interior of brick and wood. Windows are slightly canted on the inside to keep the direct light from the eyes of the congregation. Religion as harmony is the theme beautifully carried out in this church building.

Heidi Schwabacher

Christ Church Lutheran, 3244 Thirty-fourth Avenue South, Minneapolis, designed by Eliel Saarinen and his son Eero and completed in 1950.

Elbow Room

For five hours on Friday, November 15, 1974, a handsome male deer ran loose through several Minneapolis neighborhoods, interrupting a game of marbles, putting golfers off their swings, eluding police and game wardens, and finally plunging down Minnehaha Creek toward the river. When a police officer saw it running through his yard he observed wistfully, "When I go hunting I never see any deer."

That this bizarre chase ate up numerous columns of newsprint in both cities indicates that it was not an everyday occurrence. It does serve, however, to dramatize the peculiar conjunction of urban and rural life so marked in St. Paul and Minneapolis. Waterfowl as well as mosquitoes thrive on the plethora of wetlands. Cottontail rabbits are very much at home in any backyard although not so frequently spotted as the gray squirrel, which is the most commonly observed wild mammal in most yards. The so-called Minnesota gopher is actually a striped ground squirrel that can be found anywhere in short mowed grass; the true gopher, the plains pocket gopher, builds his mound home along the highways. During several summers my family and I watched an urban beaver surface into the river not very far from his lodge, apparently oblivious of the picnickers close by, overhead planes, and railroad cars clumping across the river on a nearby bridge. Several colonies of beaver have set up housekeeping farther upstream, near the university's showboat. Raccoons, weasels, and foxes have all been known to settle into city neighborhoods. The very versatile white-tailed deer often lives near residential areas on the edge of Minneapolis and St. Paul and wanders freely through a Minneapolis cemetery. This pastoral-urban mix would not be complete without those less glamorous denizens, the Norway rat and house mouse that flourish here.

The low population density partially accounts for these sights, but the fact that large amounts of land and water have been set aside for recreational areas adds to the chance of attracting and supporting wildlife. Ironically, the inner cities are themselves a wildlife sanctuary, since hunting, so avidly

Heidi Schwabacher

Resident flock of giant Canadian geese at Lake of the Isles, Minneapolis.

pursued in much of the state, is not allowed here.

By the 1960s giant Canadian geese were thought to be extinct in the Mississippi flyway, but when a few were sighted in this area an anonymous Minneapolitan asked the park department for permission to buy some additional geese and to feed and look after them. For several years this dedicated citizen seemed to be fighting a losing battle to keep the geese here, but in 1974 a number of them had survived and have remained to nest and breed at Lake of the Isles. The Park Board keeps the northwest corner of the lake open all year so that the geese can mate in winter. Just as the flock of Canadian geese took up residence in the Twin Cities after much nourishing encouragement, the park systems of both cities are the fruit of nature improved by art. Lake of the Isles itself, one of the most satisfying of our urban lakes, with its islands reserved as wildlife sanctuaries, was a mosquito-breeding swampland until the early twentieth century when, through extensive dredging, it was converted into a one-hundred-and-twenty-acre lake with eighty acres of beautifully landscaped park land. It is now one of the links in a chain of lakes, consisting also of Brownie, Cedar, and Calhoun.

The Twin Cities have too often thought of themselves as latecomers on the urban scene who must scramble to catch up with the more worldly, sophisticated eastern cities, but they were to benefit from the position of younger children in the family of American cities and in particular from the leadership of landscape architect Horace Cleveland. Like his more famous associate Frederick Law Olmsted, Cleveland was a practical radical who was urging municipalities throughout the country to acquire park lands while they were still available. It was Cleveland who designed the Roger Williams Park in Providence, Rhode Island, the grounds around the Natural Bridge in Virginia, and the Jekyll Island resort in Georgia. His park systems for Omaha and Minneapolis are cited by contemporary landscape architects as among his most outstanding achievements. Cleveland's rejection of the older system of city squares in favor of continuous open spaces lies behind the "grand rounds" parkway system in Minneapolis and the scenic boulevards in St. Paul. His philosophy of park design resembles that of the landscape architects of the English gardens in the eighteenth century, for he believed in adapting the natural features of the land to the uses of human habitation.

In 1872 Cleveland had presented plans to the St. Paul city government for a system of parks, specifically advising the city fathers to buy up the land to develop parks at Como and Phalen lakes, to set aside riverfront land for natural, unspoiled park land, and to select a prominent, commanding hill

Robert Halladay

for future state government buildings. Although neither city had as yet established a park board, Cleveland was already urging acquisition of land for an interurban boulevard along the river, foreseeing that St. Paul and Minneapolis would grow into one much larger metropolitan area which he dubbed the United Cities.

During the 1880s a small but persistent group of influential citizens pushed through the establishment of park boards in both cities and continued to work with evangelical zeal to increase and improve recreational lands. When the Minneapolis Park Board was established in 1883 Charles Loring, the first president of the board, persuaded the city to engage Cleveland as adviser. Some of the results of Cleveland's designs—Fairview, Loring, Logan, and Riverside parks—are today islands of visual relief from the lackluster streets surrounding them.

Loring, the city's Boston Common, was originally called Central Park, but was renamed for the father of Minneapolis parks. Thirty-five acres of a duck pond and marshland were reclaimed in the late nineteenth century and the park was laid out in accord with Cleveland's design. Today a nature lover would surely head first for a wilder park such as Wirth, or Crosby Nature Center in St. Paul, or one of the more refined lovelies such as Lyndale, Lake of the Isles, or Como, but Loring is a refuge for those city dwellers trapped in crowded homes and either too infirm or too poor to reach one of the more secluded parks. It is a park much used by all ages. The elderly stroll and sit, young people play basketball, and dreamers seem to be able to shut out the ever-present noise from nearby streets to gaze into the duck pond.

The old and the new meet in Loring in other ways. Near its northern perimeter is a statue of famed nineteenth-century Norwegian violinist Ole Bull, who came up the river in 1856 for the first of many visits to the Twin Cities. Both St. Paul and Minneapolis have continued to be exceptionally receptive to fine music. On the eastern edge of Loring the latest embellishment is a controversial puff-ball fountain which, although somewhat too large to be inviting, adds a feathery dimension to this old meeting place.

Acting on Cleveland's advice St. Paul acquired much of the land for Como Park in the northern part of the city in 1873, but the severe economic depression of that year and the general lack of interest in public parks contributed to a groundswell of outrage that the city should develop a park that would obviously be accessible only to the wealthy. The slowgoing horse-drawn trolleys were the only means of transportation open to the average person and it did indeed appear that only the beautiful ones would use the new park. The battle raged with a small but vocal group led by Joseph Wheel-ock, editor of the *St. Paul Pioneer Press*, in favor of keeping the Como acreage. Wheelock was an ardent proselytizer for a planned and enlarged parks system.

It was not until 1887 that money was acquired to improve Como Park and not long afterward the first Park Board was established in St. Paul. Such luminaries as General Henry Hastings Sibley and James Burbank were among its first commissioners. Wheelock was president of the board from 1893 to 1905. When one reads through the annual reports for the first few decades, Wheelock's domineering personality and willingness to resist majority pressures to skimp on park money shine through. Although a certain amount of stress is laid on the improvement of property values near developed park land, Wheelock was genuinely concerned to provide playground space for the children who found such landscape parks as Como inaccessible for everyday recreation. "In order to simplify the discipline of the playground the children were formed into a body politic, a miniature municipality, with the power to elect their own officers and have a say in the making and enforcing of their own laws. . . . One enterprising candidate for mayor formed his own party and got such a lead that no one else dared to start a party. It was also said that he promised political jobs to the available opposition candidates in addition to telling them that they had no hopes of victory. . . . All who were over eight and could read and write were allowed to vote." Wheelock observes that after the election the candidates and electorate lost all interest in directing the playground, as they were too busy playing.

Each city has its "tame" parks and lakes, often referred to as "landscape" parks, such as Highland, Phalen, and Como in St. Paul and Lake of the Isles,

Como Park Conservatory, built 1914-15, with the sculpture Crest of the Wave *by Harriet Whitney Frishmuth.*

Hiawatha, and Nokomis in Minneapolis. In both cities there are lakes with bathing beaches, swimming pools, and unfortunately too much space given over to golf courses. Como is the queen of the St. Paul park system, having received the royal treatment in the system's early days. For some years it has featured the only local zoo and a sleazy but popular midway section, but Como is largely a park of open tracts of rolling land, studded with rather formal nineteenth-century gardens and a wonderful conservatory much in the style of London's Palm House at Kew Gardens. Inside this

123

steamy place on a winter's day there is a jungle of exotic tropical plants in the rotunda. Paul Manship has produced more interesting works than his statue of the Indian boy and dog nearby, but the meandering lagoon in front is lovely. Como Park more nearly resembles European parks and the great estates of England and the Continent than do any of the other city parks, but it is a democratically welcoming place for all ages at all seasons of the year.

A wilderness area within Minneapolis, Wirth Park, has 747 acres of steep, wooded hills, rolling upland meadows, lakes, and golf courses. Mercifully, cars are not allowed within many areas although motorcyclists find the steep paths alluring and can ruin a beautiful walk. The largest of Minneapolis parks was acquired over a number of years up to 1907 and is graphic proof of the vigor of such early planners as Loring and Cleveland as well as the indefatigable Theodore Wirth, the parks superintendent for whom the park is named. For the active outdoorsman, it is the most continually surprising and satisfying open space in Minneapolis. Its hills are sometimes steep and the variety of topography is a delightful challenge. Cross-country and downhill skiing and sledding attract a number of winter sportsmen and in summer swimming is available at the not particularly pretty Wirth Lake which was part of a massive reclamation project instituted under Wirth's direction in the 1930s. During that time workers from the Civilian Conservation Corps were employed to forge a series of lagoons from large tracts of worthless swampland. Irregular in outline and of different sizes, they link Bassett's Creek with Wirth Park.

The Eloise Butler Wildflower Garden is a twenty-five-acre refuge of woods and meadows within Wirth Park. At the behest of nature lovers and teachers of botany the area was set aside and fenced in during 1907 and until 1911 was cared for voluntarily by some of its admirers. For many years a retired botany teacher, Miss Eloise Butler, served as its first curator. The prairie garden is a rolling upland meadow where the brilliant prairie wildflowers thrive in a protected but completely natural habitat. But it is the woodland area that entrances the walker; here wooded hills are banked by running myrtle, lavender bellwort, white violet, flowered trillium, wild columbine, and a variety of ferns. Plaques unobtrusively identify the plants, and birds find the whole area a sanctuary. Other walkers share the paths, but the wildflower garden is essentially an oasis within the city.

Wirth Park is one of the manifestations of the foresight of early planners, but also of the dedication of private citizens such as Miss Butler and other nature lovers who worked hard to have these areas set aside for the enjoyment of everyone before the land could become parceled out for an enclave of residential exclusivity.

If there is such a thing as an old-fashioned park, Minnehaha in Minneapolis is it, because of the large numbers of groups which use it for family and business picnics in warm weather. Most highly publicized of the festivals it attracts is that on Svenskarnas Dag, when those of Swedish descent perform native dances on a platform during a daylong celebration. Norway Day, on the second Sunday in July, is usually celebrated here too, since Minneapolis is the international headquarters for the Sons of Norway. But on any fine weekend Minnehaha attests that Twin Citians are still family people.

Most spectacular of the park's features are the famous Minnehaha Falls, which, incidentally, Longfellow never saw. Residents either tout them loud-

Eloise Butler Wildflower Garden and Prairie Garden in Theodore Wirth Park, Minneapolis.

ly or find them too boring to look at, but in wet years they are dramatic, especially in winter when they outrival any man-made sculpture. In early summer a walk along the glen below the falls reveals wildflowers such as roses and forget-me-nots, and a nearly tropical growth of trees bordering the creek as it rushes toward the Mississippi.

Within the park grounds is the John Stevens House, built in 1850. Although not originally located here, it was the first house built on the west side of the river. Across the street is the charming carpenter-Gothic Minnehaha depot, erected in

Robert Halladay

Minnehaha Depot, Minnehaha Avenue near East Forty-ninth Street, Minneapolis. This diminutive, carpenter-gothically adorned depot is often called "The Princess."

1875, a reminder of the days when the nature lover could arrive from downtown in sixteen minutes without gasoline fuming the air for a day in the park. Referring to the "numerous, varied and sometimes fantastic requests made to the park board for operating concessions within the park," Theodore Wirth reports in 1945 that "Miss Emily Ross Perry in 1891 and for a number of years after [was allowed] to sell her poem 'Minnehaha' in the Park." (Never mind the Bard of Brattle Street—he didn't live around here.)

The Minnehaha Auto Tourist Camp, established in 1921, attracted hordes of visitors every summer who lived either in their own tents or in city-built cottages. Photographs of families tenting in it in 1940 are reminders that the out-of-doors was not discovered by the generations born after World War II. But chiefly they show the conjunction of country and city within the metropolis.

It is Minnehaha Creek that is the jewel of the entire Minneapolis park system. Flowing out of Lake Minnetonka, the creek winds its way through five municipalities before it empties into the Mississippi below the falls. Seven and one half miles of it is within Minneapolis. Like all bodies of water, the creek is a creature of infinite variety, with a discreet drawing-room titter in low water, laughing a little more robustly in early summer, and reaching a Henry VIII bellow in spring seasons of particularly high water. At such times, canoeing down the creek is an amazing experience. Battling white water, the canoeist must flatten himself in his craft when high water and low bridges threaten decapitation. An eddy can reverse the canoe. When the water subsides, inner tubing down the creek is a favorite sport. And in the winter the creek valley becomes a haven for cross-country skiers.

Minnehaha Creek, Minneapolis.

Gemma Rossini Cullen

127

But all of this is in the midst of a residential area, with fine homes visible on both sides of the parkways which bound the creek and adjacent park land. In some areas the woods are fairly thick, other portions are more tamely grassed, but all are graced with the art that conceals art, a tapestry of deciduous and coniferous trees, bushes, and other plants to which a variety of birds including wild ducks are attracted. It is essentially a continuous park, a verdant ribbon decorating the southern edge of Minneapolis.

South of Marshall Avenue in St. Paul the Mississippi Boulevard takes a sudden, apparently capricious turn inland. The parkway then doubles back upon itself and rejoins the riverbank land where Summit Avenue terminates. The parkway planners wisely chose not to bridge the ravine here and as a result another wilderness within the cities was preserved as Shadow Falls Park, bordered in this case by an area of upper-middle-class homes. From either end of the twenty-acre ravine paths lead down into a thick forest. Near the farthest point inland a spring gushes out of the ground creating a clear brook running for some distance until it forms the falls at a precipitous drop. The park's name was well chosen, for even on the sunniest summer day the steepness of the ravine's sides and the dense foliage of the closely packed trees block out much of the light. Populated by numerous birds, chipmunks, wildflowers, it is another of our gems.

In the southeastern corner of St. Paul is the spectacular Battle Creek Park with its canyon entrance of white friable St. Peter sandstone, which is composed of pitted or frosted windblown sand grains deposited in Ordovician seas forty million years ago. Battle Creek, in 1842 the site of one of the last battles between the Chippewa and the Sioux, has dangerously steep paths but is a wonderful alternative to the landscape parks. The coniferous and birch and other deciduous trees crowd the steep hills which converge onto the creek. Unfortunately, this is the only major creek left of a number that existed in St. Paul. Over the years Battle Creek has been nearly destroyed by the building of industrial plants and a highway and the filling in of Battle Creek Lake. But the remainder of the creek is within one of the more dramatic of the half-wild parks in the Twin Cities. In the cliffs are a number of small caves, not deep enough to be dangerous. On a weekend afternoon it is not unusual to imagine the guerrilla techniques of the Sioux and Chippewa, for young persons of rock-throwing age enjoy pelting the walkers from the cliffs. It is not surprising that in nearby residential sections we find ourselves slowing down the car for tame geese waddling along the road.

If any additional proof were needed that the Twin Cities offer wilderness within an urban area, there is the Crosby Farm Park and nature center in St. Paul which lies between Highways 5 and 35 along the Mississippi. The name derives from the Crosby Farm, located originally at the far eastern end of the park. Eight miles of pathways, including a bog trail between two lakes, wend their way through a part of the five hundred and four acres. A sizable number of deer come and go within the Crosby Farm. Smaller animals such as woodchucks, raccoons, rabbits, squirrels, and a variety of birds live there permanently in great numbers. The most unusual feature about the Crosby Farm is the feeling of total wilderness, for although it is within a few miles of downtown St. Paul and close to residential areas, there are almost no visible traces of civilization, except the paved paths. The park en-

Battle Creek Park, St. Paul.

Robert N. Taylor

129

Robert Halladay

compasses open swamp areas, deep woodlands, and some Renoir fields of yellow, blue, and purple wildflowers.

Minneapolis has 5,500 acres of park land, 1,400 of which are water. St. Paul's system has 2,600 acres. In both cities park land is made up of playgrounds, parkways, triangles, larger parks, golf courses.

Digging into the actual history of particular parks often reveals a tale of citizens battling for years for acquisition or expansion of open space to meet needs. It is too often the case that overcrowded neighborhoods where parents have neither the time nor the energy to attend meetings are the very communities which most need playspace. In Minneapolis the Model City area—bounded roughly by Thirty-sixth Street and Lyndale, Franklin, and Cedar avenues—had a poor ratio of park property to people, although recently land acquisition is setting this to rights. The Prospect Park neighborhood in Southeast Minneapolis was already deficient in open space when the federally subsidized Glendale Homes were built in the early 1950s, adding approximately 600 children under the age of eighteen to the neighborhood. In 1957 Luxton Field, a five-acre tract adjacent to the Glendale Project, was threatened with near extinction when the Highway Department drew up plans to build a stretch of Interstate 94. The Prospect Park and East River Road Association, an unusually vigorous neighborhood group, struggled through an exhausting number of meetings, ultimately salvaging part of the playground area by convincing the Highway Department to construct a wall rather than a slope along the strip adjacent to the park. At that time, neighborhood associations were required under the now defunct Elwell Law to acquire signatures of fifty-one

Heidi Schwabacher

Crosby Farm Park, a wilderness along the Mississippi in St. Paul.

percent of the residents asking for such a change, and residents had to be assessed for a large portion of the funds for rehabilitation. This meant getting in touch with and persuading absentee landlords, often a difficult task. But the goal was achieved and the inadequate park was rehabilitated with a handsome neighborhood recreation center and an increase in play equipment. It is not a particularly pretty park and an implacable roar from the freeway makes it a depressing place for anyone seeking quiet, but the rehabilitation was worth the effort as a large number of children and adults make use of the playing fields, wading pool, and recreation center.

On the northside of St. Paul, Marydale Park was developed out of Loeb Lake, a dumping ground, and the acreage surrounding it in the mid 1970s. More than a decade of pressure on City Hall was required before neighborhood residents saw this wasteland refurbished into a handsome hilly park of twenty-two acres. It is a much needed ornament in a neighborhood where yards are small and where nearby railroad tracks do little to beautify the area. The happy ending to such a story is not always possible, and in neighborhoods where residents do not remain for long periods of time the chances of effecting change are slim.

After the residents of Swede Hollow were evicted in 1956 East Side citizens urged the city government to convert the more than twenty acres into a park, but the hollow was actually used for a dumping ground for a number of years. The combination of refuse and caves in the hollow's banks made it a particularly dangerous attraction for children. When a boy was killed in a cave in 1964 outraged citizens succeeded in persuading the city government to seal off the caves, but it was not until the 1970s, when the Dayton's Bluff Community Council successfully halted the construction of a highway overpass that would have bridged Swede Hollow, that the city agreed to convert the historic ravine into a park.

The Minneapolis Park Board has been gradually shifting its focus to social and recreational use of parks, with less stress on the highly physical athletic programs of earlier years. Neighborhood park councils, apparently unique to Minneapolis, have been evolving since the early 1950s and on the whole present a healthy kind of leadership since needs of a particular community can most accurately be assessed by the residents. They are a liaison group between residents and the Park Board. Of course the quality of leadership depends on a kaleidoscope of factors since residents of certain communities tend to have more time and expertise in working with and running councils than do those in others. Similarly neighborhood sports programs are unevenly dependent upon the generosity of local businessmen for uniforms and equipment.

The Recreational Division of the St. Paul Park Board also stresses leisure activities for all ages rather than highly vigorous team sports. Each of its fifty-two neighborhood centers has its own program and usually a full-time person in charge, but volunteer help and dependence on booster clubs to raise money for equipment means disparate recreational opportunities.

Too much of the wild and natural riverbank property is a tantalizing prize within sight but out of reach of the majority of residents where the banks are highly precipitous, and in only a few areas have even rudimentary steps been constructed. St. Paul has made somewhat better use of its riverfront possibilities than has Minneapolis. Hidden Falls

Park, for example, can be reached by car. A tangle of wild grapevines runs along a sandy shore, gnarled roots of trees are exposed, and although the St. Paul Park Department has spruced up the wilderness with a few amenities, such as a picnic pavilion and a bridge over the creek, paths lead through still unspoiled woods. It is a wildlife sanctuary, although some unwanted forms of wildlife such as motorbikes find their way into this city wilderness.

One of the most precipitous and ruggedly beautiful stretches of the riverbank runs from the Franklin Avenue Bridge to the river flats upstream in Minneapolis. The section of the West River Road along here was completed as late as 1940. It was a particularly challenging stretch of the riverbank for boulevard builders, as it involved draining systems, land walls, fencing, handrails, and a great deal of grading. It is a late manifestation of Horace Cleveland's vision of the urban-rural continuum, a rugged clifflike section at its most beautiful when the configurations of ice cling to it for many winter months. Here too at the river's edge in the fishing season a sprinkling of loyal fishermen can be found, for surprisingly the river flows relatively clear through Minneapolis. Northern pike, crappies, and small mouth bass are abundant in the Mississippi. This is only a fraction of the many miles of lake and river open to shore fishing in the cities.

As part of the seven-county Metropolitan Council, Minneapolis and St. Paul are participants in an unusual open-space program, put into operation in 1974 by the Metropolitan Parks Act. Under this law there was established a system of regional parks, which are used by residents from a number of communities. Major park agencies, the state legislature, and the Metropolitan Council work together to identify and develop regional open-space areas. Certain

Heidi Schwabacher

The many outdoor skating areas attract skaters of all ages in both cities.

older parks such as Theodore Wirth and the lake parks in Minneapolis and Como Park in St. Paul which have long attracted people from other cities and counties have been designated regional parks and as such are eligible for redevelopment with funds from the Metropolitan Council. The council acquires no land, but instead awards funds to a government unit to buy land which has been designated suitable for a regional park. Thus, part of the town of Lilydale on the Mississippi River was acquired and developed into public riverfront open space by the Ramsey County Park Board. The recognition

Hidden Falls Park, St. Paul. Exposed tree roots reveal the ravages of spring floods along the banks of the Mississippi.

that many larger parks are used by residents from a wide area and the opportunities that this law provides for securing land for everyone rather than the select few significantly augment the open spaces available for Twin Citians as well as their neighbors. The possibilities that this program provides for recreation within or close to the cities in an era of rapidly diminishing energy supplies are immense.

Open spaces are more than the sum of parks and recreation departments in any city. Often cemeteries and college campuses extend the available breathing space. Ironically, Minneapolis, which has one of the largest public universities in the nation, has a particularly drab campus and one which does little to enhance the Southeast section of the city. With a University of Virginia style Forum Romanum designed by Cass Gilbert and an interesting collection of nineteenth- and early-twentieth-century eclectic style buildings, the campus was chiefly distinguished for its fine landscaping and well-cared-for grounds. But with the influx of students after World War II a raft of temporary buildings were thrown up on the East Bank Campus in barracks-style structures. Since then permanent buildings have gradually replaced the temporary sheds, some of which reached the ripe old age of twenty-five years before being torn down. Some of the new buildings are four- to eight-story basements, a few cuts above Temporary North of Child Welfare and Temporary South of Mines. In the 1970s an ungainly Health Science Tower rose to crouch over it all in menacing fashion. To paraphrase John Dryden, this campus "never deviates into sense."

As for the newer campus on the west bank of the river, concretized fill between buildings of the handy-for-gunning-down-street-revolutionaries style seems to be the order of the day, although the landscape designers have made good use of the riverbank.

The small colleges of St. Paul grew up in a period of ample space and were not under the same pressure to build, build, build as the university. Even the University of Minnesota campus in St. Paul has grown more gracefully than its Minneapolis counterpart although it was not gifted with the beautiful river site in Minneapolis. In the same neighborhood, the Luther Theological Seminary resides on rolling hills, and a generous amount of land is given to Vermont maples, oaks, elms, and coniferous trees.

Old Muskego Church, the first Norwegian Lutheran church building in this country, was moved here from Wisconsin in the early years of this century. In its plain unfinished siding, within a particularly lovely stand of Norway pines, it is a quietly stern reminder of more spartan days.

Where Summit Avenue meets the Mississippi Boulevard it is flanked by the steep Shadow Falls ravine and the campus of the St. Paul Seminary. A hushed Old World monastic atmosphere pervades the campus, where cassocked priests stroll contemplatively through the generous expanse of tree-studded grounds. At the top of the rise, somewhat softened by trees, a neo-Romanesque chapel intensifies the European atmosphere. The campus has been beautifully endowed with conifers. Farther along Summit Avenue are the somewhat traditional yellow-limestone Gothic buildings of the College of St. Thomas. Although none of the buildings is particularly distinguished, the wide expanse of lawn reinforces the feeling of open space for the neighborhood.

The gem of the Twin Cities college campuses is that of the College of St. Catherine in St. Paul, bounded by Cleveland, Randolph, Bayard, and Fairview avenues. One of the finest man-made landscapes in the cities, it has a rolling grassy area which slopes down to a charming duck pond. An intact woodland has been preserved as part of the campus. Buildings range from the early twentieth century to a latter-day Breueresque Fine Arts Center, which has a particularly handsome interior.

Neither Macalester College nor Hamline University can compete with St. Kate's, but both offer open spaces with congenial buildings for St. Paulites in their neighborhoods.

Relief from the more cheerless sections of the in-

Robert N. Taylor

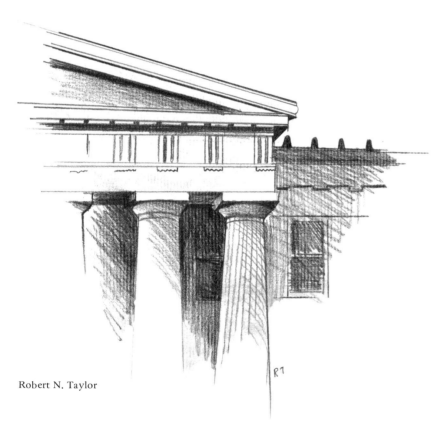

Robert N. Taylor

ner city is found in cemeteries such as the Minneapolis Pioneers and Soldiers Memorial Cemetery (often called Laymans Cemetery) at the corner of Cedar Avenue and Lake Street. It was opened in 1858 and contains the graves of many of the city's early settlers. John T. Hoblit, the first Minnesotan to die in the Civil War, Philander Prescott, married to an Indian and killed at the start of the Sioux uprising in 1862, and Charles Christmas, the surveyor who laid out the city streets, are all buried here. The cracked gravestones tell us much of the origins of early Minneapolis residents. Here are the Andersens, Sorensons, Ludwigs, Valborgs, Bolstads, and Johnsons. This oasis of heavily wooded and grassed-in land provides a parklike setting in a particularly depressing commercial and residential area of Minneapolis.

Oakland Cemetery is a peaceful retreat near a sad-looking neighborhood in the north end of St. Paul. It is a beautifully cared-for tract of gently rolling, heavily wooded land dating back to 1853 as a burial ground. Gravestones range from simple stone plaques to imposing tombs and the names—Hartwig, Wermuth, Siebert, Schmid, Wold, Schaefer, Morphy, and Armstrong—tell us something of the St. Paul mix. How ironic that the living are condemned to Sylvan Street when the dead have an elegantly appointed park!

When the big sky, lakes, river, and man-made structures work together in a successful composition it is easy to fall into a Wordsworthian "earth has not anything to show more fair" reverie, but when a congeries of junkyards, railroad tracks, blinking bottle caps, and billboards assault the eye, these are the cities of dreadful night. It would be false to proclaim St. Paul and Minneapolis garden cities ornamented with remarkable buildings. Much

136

Details from three nineteenth-century buildings, University of Minnesota, east bank campus, Minneapolis: Upper left, Eddy Hall, built 1885-86, oldest surviving University building. Lower left, Burton Hall, Greek revival of the 1890s. Right, Pillsbury Hall, designed by the firm of L. S. Buffington, built 1887-90, in fortresslike Richardsonian Romanesque style.

Heidi Schwabacher

College of St. Catherine, St. Paul, looking from Dew Drop Pond toward Italianate chapel and campanile.

of the architecture is drab and some of the most interesting buildings lie hidden in a wasteland. Ten-minute waits for railroad cars to back and fill and hitch up their stays in public—always it seems when the temperature is ninety-five or in the middle of a blizzard at the end of a tiring day—do little to beautify or endear this metropolis to anyone.

Yet there is still ample visual and psychological elbowroom here. The roar of freeway traffic penetrating an inner-city yard is mitigated by tomatoes and snapdragons growing, many-hued butterflies and cardinals moving, and the mesmerizing bonk of tennis balls from a public court half a block away. You can see the sky without an intervening scrim of smog most days. You can go to Orchestra Hall or a debate at the statehouse without making elaborate preparations ahead of time. Kids learn to trav-el from one end of the metropolitan area to another at an early age, grow up fishermen, boaters, and connoisseurs of art and theater. The Farmers Market purveys fruit, vegetables, and flowers in the open air a few minutes north of downtown Minneapolis. This region of little heavy industry has been spared the most unsightly urban visual blight and livable neighborhoods offer residents an identity.

A few years ago a Cockney friend remarked after several months of exile from his own beloved metropolis, "Call this a city? Why, I've seen squirrels running through the downtown streets!" He could have been talking of either Minneapolis or St. Paul; in many respects they are big small towns. What the cities provide is not always remarkable, not always desirable. But the best qualities are easily accessible to residents and visitors alike.

Gemma Rossini Cullen

Left, the Mississippi River near downtown St. Paul. Right, looking downriver in Minneapolis near the Franklin Avenue Bridge.

Index

143

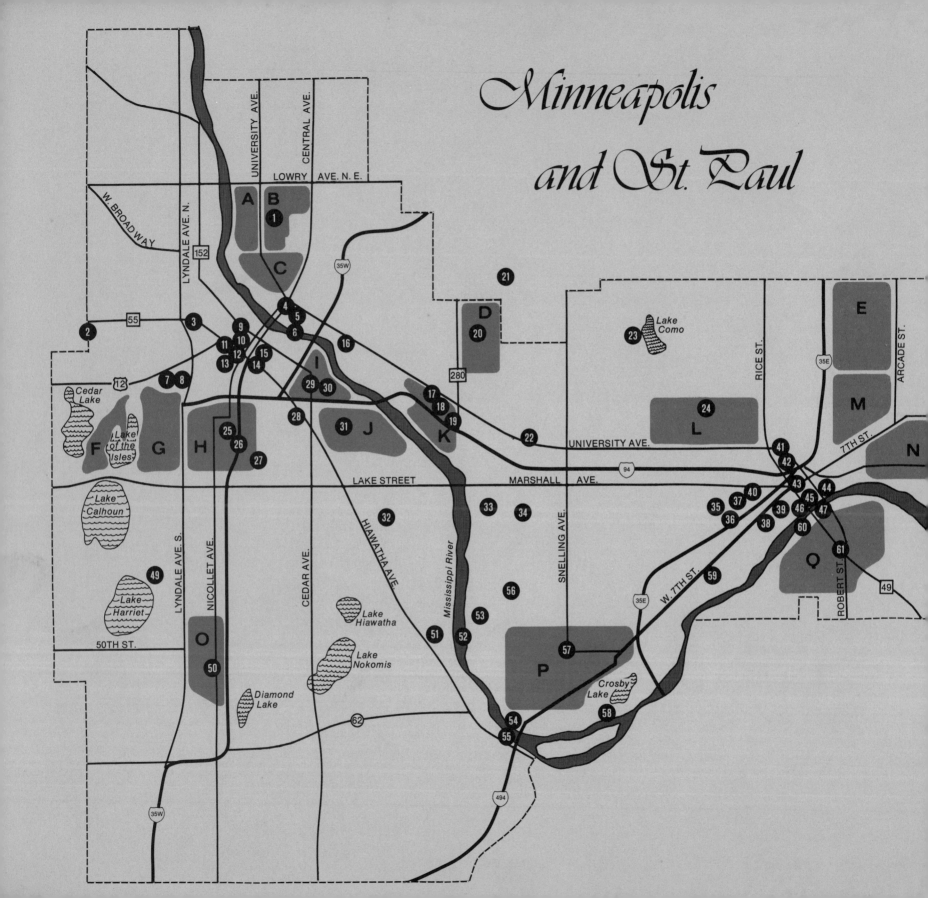